THE ANGELS AND THEIR MISSION

According to the Fathers of the Church

THE ANGELS AND
THEIR MISSION

by JEAN DANIELOU

translated from the French by

DAVID HEIMANN

Christian Classics™

A DIVISION OF THOMAS MORE PUBLISHING

Allen, Texas

Originally published in 1953 as
Les Anges et Leur Mission
by
Editions de Chevetogne
Chevetogne, Belgium

Nihil Obstat: Edward A. Cerny, S.S., D.D.
Censor Librorum

Imprimatur: Francis P. Keough, D.D.
Archbishop of Baltimore
October 15, 1956

Send all inquiries to:
CHRISTIAN CLASSICS™
a Division of Thomas More Publishing
200 East Bethany Drive
Allen, Texas 75002-3804

BOOKSTORES:
  Call Bookworld Companies 888-444-2524 or fax 941-753-9396
PARISHES AND SCHOOLS:
  Thomas More Publishing 800-822-6701 or fax 800-688-8356
INTERNATIONAL:
  Fax Thomas More Publishing 972-264-3719

Printed in the United States of America

Library of Congress Catalog Card Number 56-11414

ISBN 0-87061-056-2

5 6 7 8 9   04 03 02 01 00

◄§ Contents §►

Introduction

To devote an entire book to the subject of angels might
seem at first glance unwarranted. But the question is not
without its practical value. There is a passage in the Encyclical *Humani Generis* which expresses concern over the fact
that many people today deny the personal character of the
celestial spirits. And indeed there are two chief errors concerning this subject. The first comes from the rationalists
who group angels and demons together as personifications of
psychological realities and who would like to see in them a
mythical interpretation of data to which psychoanalysis
would furnish the key. Others, justifiably reacting against
these tendencies, show a lively interest in the invisible world;
but they seek to penetrate it by means of spiritism or theos-

ophy, and, by their imprudent attempts, they stray from the one single way of access which is given to us, Jesus Christ.

That is why it will not be inopportune to speak of the angels. It might be noted further that the greatest among the saints and men of God, from St. Augustine to John Henry Newman, have always lived on familiar terms with them. And the tradition of the Church has always accorded them a very large place in her theology. It is enough to recall the lengthy articles devoted to them in the *Summa theologica* of St. Thomas, where the most subtle questions concerning their nature and their grace, their intellect and their love are solved with an admirable mastery.

It has often seemed to us as we read the Fathers of the Church, that the circumstances of their times drew their attention to several questions which later theologians have felt no need to examine at any great length. In angelology, their attention was focused less upon the nature of the angels and their function as adoring spirits than upon their missions to humanity at different moments in the history of salvation.

In this, moreover, they were simply the exegetes of Sacred Scripture. The Bible shows us Almighty God using "ministering spirits" (Hebr. 1:14) throughout the whole of the Old Testament, making them the messengers of His revelations. On the threshold of the New Testament it is once again the angels who instruct Zachary, Joseph and Mary in the mysteries of the coming of the Son of God. The Apocalypse of St. John shows them presiding over the growth and development of the Church. And all of Scripture proclaims their participation in the glories of the Second Coming.

Surrounded by a variety of vastly different social and intellectual cultures, it was the office of the Fathers to recognize in each of them whatever it professed of truth, and, placing each in its proper perspective in the light of rising Christianity, to render more accessible to men of every culture the truths of Christ's Church.

The Christian doctrine of the angels is, first of all, a continuation of their appearance in the Jewish religion of the Old Testament. But the existence of ministers intermediate between God and man fitted itself with advantage into the spreading philosophical systems of Neo-Platonism, the occult religious systems of the Orient which had long plagued the empire, and even the Roman mind itself with its pantheon of greater and lesser deities.

There came a time, however, when, with the fusion of these divergent cultures, and the rise of specific and more fundamental controversial questions, the attention of churchmen was centered elsewhere and a lively interest in the world of the created spirits was no longer either possible or necessary. Thus, much of what the Fathers treated with special attention later theological developments have bypassed.

This was neither inevitable nor unforeseen. There are those who see in the patristic treatment of the missions of the angels merely a crowning example of what they have come to regard as the "naïveté of the early Church writers." But there is a vital and fundamental distinction between naïveté and genuine fervor and piety. To fail to realize this is to have misunderstood not only the Fathers and the missions of the angels but the spirit of the Church as well.

The perspective we have adopted—the role of the angels in the economy of salvation—forced us to follow a historical order. This has the inconvenience of making us begin with the most austere part of the subject, that which concerns the role of the angels in the world before the coming of

Christ. It would have been more appealing to our readers had we begun with the activity of the angels in those of their ministrations which are most familiar to us, and shown them first of all announcing the gospel to the shepherds, consoling Christ in His agony, watching over the souls of the baptized, aiding the hermits in their temptations, leading the saints to paradise, and raising the dead from the tomb. But we would not fully understand the joyous hymns with which they greet the comings of Christ unless we had first shared in their patience during the advent of their waiting.

THE ANGELS AND THEIR MISSION

◄§ 1 §►

The Angels and the Law

A study of the missions of the angels which is to follow rigorously the order of their intervention in the world as instruments of Divine Providence would have to begin with their action in the physical world, the activity which preceded their missions among men. Athenagoras says that "the Demiurge and Creator of the world, God, through the medium of His Word, has apportioned and ordained the angels to occupy the elements, the heavens, the world, and whatever is in the world." [1] Origen speaks of angels set in charge of the four elements, who were perhaps well known to St. Paul (Gal. 4:9), and of angels presiding over the different

[1] *Suppl.*, 10.

domains of the universe, over the stars, the meteors, the plants and the animals.[2] St. Thomas Aquinas, moreover, confirms this as a traditional teaching: "All corporeal things are governed by the angels. And this is not only the teaching of the holy doctors, but of all the philosophers."[3]

This, then, is a doctrine which is solidly established in tradition and in reason. With all due deference to the rationalism of certain of our contemporaries, the intelligent and forceful government to which the order of the universe bears witness might very easily have heavenly spirits as its ministers. This bond between the angels and the visible universe, furthermore, could very well give us the key to certain mysteries. But there is nothing to be gained in beginning this study with a thought so bold that it would startle even the best disposed readers and perhaps keep them from taking seriously the more important things that will be mentioned later. Besides, our subject is limited to the study of the mission of angels among men. It is in the measure that they assist man in the pursuit of his final end that they are the ministers of the gifts of God in the natural order as well as in the supernatural. [4]

Thus, this chapter begins, not with the role of the angels in the material world, nor even with their role among primitive man, but rather with their relation to that great event which is properly called the beginning of the history of salvation—the election of the people of Israel. The idea that Israel was the object of particular assistance from the angels comes from the Old Testament and from the Jewish tradi-

[2] *Hom. 10 in Jer.*, 6. See also Apoc. 14:7. On the Judaistic origin of these concepts see Bietenhard, *Die himmlische Welt im Urchristentum und Spaetjudentum*, Tuebingen (1951), pp. 101 ff.

[3] *ST*, 1, 110, 1.

[4] This is how they are envisaged in Hebrews 1:14.

tion. The Book of Daniel shows the Archangel Michael as
the protector of the Jewish people (Dan. 10:13-21; 12:1).
This belief is found again in the Jewish literature,[5] and the
Christians developed it further.[6] Pseudo-Dionysius echoes
this tradition. "Theology," he says, "calls Michael the angel
of the people of Israel." [7]

This assistance of the angels to the Jewish people finds
expression first of all in the fact that they are ministers of
the revelations of God. An angel promises to Abraham that
he will be the father of a numerous posterity (Gen. 22:
15-18); the wife of Manue learns from an angel that she
will have a son (Judges 13:3). The angels also come to
strengthen the servants of God in the accomplishment of
their tasks (3 Kings 19:5). But the Jewish tradition and
later, the Christian authors are not content with these few
details. They maintain that the whole economy of the Old
Testament was communicated to the Jews through the medium of the angels. Clement of Alexandria explains that
there are protoctist [or first-operating] angels, who effect
these covenants through the medium of other angels. [8] Thus
"Abraham was initiated into the secrets of God by an
angel." [9]

The outstanding instance of this role of the angels in the
transmission of the Old Covenant is the communication of
the Law. This was a popular doctrine in pre-Christian Judaism. The Greek translation of Deuteronomy (33:2), where
the development of angelology can be seen so clearly, al-

[5] W. Luecken, *Michael*, pp. 17-20.
[6] See Hermas, *Shepherd*, Sim. 8, 2, 3.
[7] *Hier. coel.*, 9, 2.
[8] *Eclog.*, 51. See also *Strom.*, 7, 2.
[9] *Strom.*, 5, 11. See Hilary, *Tract. Ps. 118*; *Tract. Ps. 121*; Eusebius, *Praep. Ev.*, 7, 5; Methodius, *De sanguisuga*, 7. "It is an
angel who reveals the hidden things to Daniel, Ezechiel, Zachary, and all the prophets."

ludes to their presence on Sinai. In place of "The Lord came from Sinai; from his right hand there sprang forth rays of light," the Greek text reads, "At his right hand the angels accompanied him." The *Book of Jubilees* shows Jahweh confiding to the angel of the presence (who is probably Michael, the protector angel of Israel) the composition and promulgation of the Law. "Jahweh said to the angel of the presence, 'Write for Moses since the beginning of creation up unto the building of my sanctuary among them for eternity.'" [10] This is found again in Josephus: "It is from God, through angels, that we have learned the most beautiful of our doctrines and the most holy sections of our laws." [11]

This same concept is found in Christian tradition. St. Paul already mentions it in the Epistle to the Galatians: "Why then was the Law? It was enacted on account of transgressions, being delivered by angels through a mediator" (3:19). In the Acts of the Apostles Stephen declares, "You have received the Law as an ordinance of angels and have not kept it" (7:53). And the Epistle to the Hebrews speaks of "the word promulgated by the angels," to designate the Mosaic Law in opposition to "the message announced by the Lord" (2:2-3).

This idea is also found in the Fathers. St. Hilary says: "Among the [Jewish] people there was a spiritual watch at that time by which the administration of the Law procured through the angels was safeguarded." [12] The Law appeared as one aspect of the "watch" of the angels over Israel. Elsewhere, St. Hilary, commenting on Psalm 67, shows the angel hosts present on Sinai for the promulgation of the

[10] *Jub.*, 1, 27.
[11] *Ant. Jud.*, 15, 5, 3. See Strack-Billerbeck 3, 544 ff.
[12] *Tract. Ps.* 54. See also *Tract. Ps.* 67; *Tract. Ps.* 137; Methodius, *De sang.*, 7.

Law. "These burning torches, these dazzling fires, these rumbling thunders, this terror which accompanies the entire coming of the Lord—all manifest the presence of the angelic ministers, setting down the Law through the hand of a mediator." [13] Augustine will also write: "The angels proclaimed the Law with an awesome voice." [14] This is an echo of the Jewish traditions attested to in the Greek version of Deuteronomy quoted above.

Pseudo-Dionysius summarizes the entire tradition in his *Celestial Hierarchy.* "Just as theology teaches, the Law was transmitted to us by the angels. In the days before the Law, just as under the Law itself, it was the angels who guided our revered ancestors toward the divine realities, either by prescribing the rules for their conduct, or, as interpreters, by revealing to them the holy ordinances, the secret vision of mysteries that are not of this world, or various prophecies. Some may object, 'Scriptural tradition affirms that the holy precepts of the Law were transmitted directly by God Himself to Moses.' We answer that this is said in order to make it absolutely impossible for us to forget that these prescriptions are really the image of the divine and sacred Law. But theology wisely teaches that these prescriptions have come to us through the intermediary of the angels, so that the very order instituted by the divine Legislator might show us that inferior beings are to rise spiritually toward the divine through the intermediary of beings who are hierarchically superior." [15]

If the promulgation of the Law is the principal gift made by God to His people through the ministry of the angels, it is not the only one. Origen writes that "the angels served the people of Israel in the Law and in the other mysteries." [16] Thus it is that, according to St. Hilary, the manna was given

[13] *Tract. Ps. 67.*   [14] *Civ. Dei,* 10, 15. See also 10, 17.
[15] *Hier. coel.,* 4, 2, 3.   [16] *Comm. in Cant.,* 2.

by the angels. "The Law was promulgated by the angels, and man has eaten the bread of angels, and the heavens are said to have diffused their dew on Sinai; certainly it is by the heavens—that is to say, by the angels—that the manna was bestowed on Sinai." [17]

This, as the Book of Wisdom testifies, rests again upon the traditions of Alexandrian Judaism. "Thou didst feed thy people with the food of angels and gavest them bread from heaven prepared without labor, having in it all that is delicious and the sweetness of every taste" (Wis. 16:20). According to Hilary, moreover, Israel was served by the angels during the entire time of the Exodus. [18] That is no doubt why we see Christ, the true Israel, being served by angels in the desert after the forty days of temptation, which correspond to the forty years of the Exodus (Mark 1:13). And this will remain true, in the Church, of all those who leave Egypt behind them and set out across the desert toward the mountain of the vision. Origen says, "Do not waver at the solitude of the desert; it is during your sojourn in the tents that you will receive the manna from heaven and eat the bread of angels." [19]

This assistance of the angels with respect to Israel concerns not only the communication of divine goods but also their conservation. Saint Hilary speaks of the *custodia*, the spiritual watch which was entrusted to them. For him, not only is the communication of the Law made by the angels, but even its administration is in their hands. [20] Thus, there was an angel who watched over the Law and, until the time of Christ, assured its authentic interpretation. This is also true of the Temple. Origen tells us that the "Ark of the

[17] *Tract. Ps. 67.* See also Eusebius, *Comm. in Ps. 77.*
[18] *Comm. in Matt.*, 3:1.
[19] Origen, *Hom. 17 in Num.*, 3.
[20] *Tract. Ps. 54.*

Covenant, the mercy seat, the Cherubim, and even the temple itself" were given to Israel through the angels. [21] Besides that, an angel watched over the holiness of the Temple. Perhaps it was he who flogged Heliodorus when he tried to force his way into the Holy of Holies. This angelic protection is accorded the Temple as long as the presence of God abides there and is withdrawn when, at the death of Christ, the Temple becomes a thing of the past and the veil is lifted. Meliton of Sardis alludes to this truth, [22] and St. Hilary is even more explicit: "And then [at the crucifixion] . . . the honor of the veil together with the watch of the protector angel is withdrawn." [23]

This last text leads to an important remark on the meaning of the ministry of the angels among the people of Israel. For the Jews, it is connected with a general order of things in which the role of the angels is that of intermediary between God and men. Pseudo-Dionysius holds the same view. The early Christian view, however, is different. According to it, the role of the angels in the Old Testament is bound up with the Old Testament's preparatory mission, and it ceases with the coming of Christ, who takes the history of salvation directly into His own hands. This certainly seems to have been the view of St. Paul. In the texts cited above he opposes the communication of the Law through the angels to the revelation of the Gospel through Christ. This is particularly stressed in the Epistle to the Hebrews: "For He has

[21] *Comm. in Cant.*, 2.

[22] *Homily on the Pascha*, 98.

[23] *Comm. in Matt.*, 33:7. See also *Tract. Ps. 59.* For Eusebius there is question of several angels. *Frag. Luc.* See also *Comm. in Is.*, 1. It is remarkable that the Jewish tradition in its turn reports that the angels abandoned the Temple after its destruction by Titus in 70. *Ap. Baruch*, 6, 7; 8, 2; Josephus, *Bell. Jud.*, 6, 5, 3. It is possible that the Christian tradition is a transposition of the Jewish.

not subjected to angels the world to come, whereof we speak.
. . . But, in subjecting all things to him, he left nothing
that is not subject to him" (2:5-8).

It also seems that the Epistle to the Galatians should be
interpreted in the same way: "As long as the heir is a child,
he is under guardians and stewards. So we too, when we were
children, were enslaved under the elements of the world. But
when the fulness of time came, God sent his Son" (4:1-6).
A comparison with Colossians 2:8 ("See to it that no one
deceive you by philosophy and vain deceit, according to human traditions, according to the elements of the world and
not according to Christ") would seem to imply the presence
of angels here. But this last epistle treats of the dispossession
of the angels by Christ at His coming. It does not seem that
there is any allusion to evil angels in these passages, but
merely to angels who have, so to speak, passed out of date
so that their cult (a practice for which they are not responsible) constitutes an anachronism, just as culpable, now that
Christ has come, as is the observance of the Law which they
promulgated. [24]

This view of St. Paul's is developed by Origen in his commentary on the Canticle of Canticles. The friends of the
Bridegroom are the angels who instruct the Church—that
is to say, the people of God—during the time of their es-
pousals, the Old Testament. But the Church longs for the
kiss of the Bridegroom, His coming in person. "When I was
preparing myself for my marriage with the Son of the King

[24] See Chrysostom, *Hom. in Col.*, 2:7. After speaking of those
who keep the Jewish feasts, he adds, "They say that we have to
be guided by angels, and not by Christ." Certain pejorative expressions used by St. Paul with regard to the Powers, words
which might lead one to believe that he is speaking of demons,
are no different than those he uses with regard to the Law which
is nonetheless of divine institution. See L. Cerfaux, *Le Christ
dans la théologie de saint Paul*, 1951, p. 169.

and the first-born of every creature, the holy angels followed me and ministered to me, bringing me the Law as a wedding present. Indeed it has been said that the Law was promulgated through the angels by means of a mediator (Gal. 3:19). But, since the world was already nearing its end and still His presence was not granted me and I only saw His servants rising and descending about me, I poured out my prayer to you, the Father of my Bridegroom, begging you to have pity on my love and send Him to me so that He need no longer speak with me through His servants the angels but might come Himself." [25]

This parallelism between the Old Testament and the angels on the one hand and the New Testament and Christ on the other is developed by Origen in commenting on the Canticle 1:10. "We will make thee chains of gold, inlaid with silver." This time he sets it in relation with the figurative character of the Old Law, which is signified by the silver, as opposed to the spiritual reality of the Gospel, which is the gold. "We propose to show how the holy angels who, before the coming of Christ, watched over the bride while she was still young are the friends and companions of the Bridegroom mentioned here. . . . In fact, it seems to me that the Law which was promulgated through the agency of a mediator did indeed contain a foreshadowing of the good things which were to come, but not their actual likeness; and that the events set down in the Law and enacted in figure though not in reality are merely imitations of gold, not real gold.

"Among these imitations are the Ark of the Covenant, the mercy seat, the Cherubim, . . . the Temple itself and everything which is written in the Law. It is these imitations which were given to the Church, the bride, by the angels, who are the friends of the Bridegroom and who served her

[25] *Comm. in Cant.*, 1.

in the Law and the other mysteries. That, I believe, is what
St. Paul meant when he spoke of the 'worship of the angels
which some enter into blindly, puffed up by their mere human minds' (Col. 2:18). Thus, the entire cult and the religion of the Jews were imitations of the gold. Whenever
anyone turns toward the Lord and the veil is lifted from before him, he sees the real gold." [26]

It is remarkable that Origen links this very passage in
Colossians to the matter under discussion. For him, the cult
of the angels mentioned there is merely another name for
Judaism itself, inasmuch as it was promulgated by the
angels. This constitutes an exegesis of St. Paul quite in accord with what has been said above and leads to the conclusion that this economy, like any preparation, was essentially
provisional. "That which was procured through the angels,
since it was only an imitation of the gold, did not have the
promise of lasting forever. Rather, a time was set for it by
the angels themselves when they said that these things were
being given for as long as 'the King is at his repose.'" [27]

One final point of interest in this interpretation of Origen's is the parallelism which he sets up between the role of
the angels in the historical preparation of Christ and their
role in the first formation of the soul. "If we explain the
passage as referring to the soul, it must appear that, as long
as the soul is still young and not fully formed, it is under
guardians and teachers. These are the angels who are called
the guardians of children and who always see the face of the
Father in heaven. Accordingly, they are imitations of gold

[26] *Ibid.*, 2.
[27] *Ibid.* Thus the ministry of the angels has always been to prepare the coming of Christ. "The Father has sent His angels to announce the coming of Christ. For if it is through the angels that
the Law is given to Moses, that Law announced Christ." Methodius, *De sang.*, 7.

given to the soul which is not yet sustained with the solid nourishment of the Word." [28] Thus there is a parallelism between the history of humanity and the history of the individual. In the one as well as the other, the role of the angels is concerned with the beginnings, the preparations. This conception contains an entire general theology of the missions of the angels in outline form.

[28] *Ibid.*

2

The Angels and the World Religion

The communication of covenants and of the Law represents an outstanding gift of God to the people of Israel made through the intermediary of the angels. But this does not mean that the other peoples living before the coming of Christ were completely deprived of divine assistance and excluded from the whole process of preparation. Prior to the covenant with Abraham the Old Testament knew an earlier alliance, that of Noe, contracted with the whole of humanity. Its object was the fidelity of God in regard to the world and its symbol was the rainbow. This is the covenant which is spoken of in the Acts of the Apostles (14:16). "In the generations that are past he let all the nations follow their own ways, and yet He did not leave Himself without testimony, bestowing blessings, giving rains from heaven and fruitful seasons, filling their hearts with good and gladness." Thus, the very regularity of the laws of nature is a sort of revelation through which man can recognize the existence of a provident God. That is the teaching of the Epistle to the Romans (1:20): "Since the creation of the world his invisible attributes are clearly seen, being understood through the things that are made."

In this divine assistance to the nations the angels also have a role to play. It is, in fact, a common doctrine in the whole of ancient tradition that God has entrusted the nations to His angels. This doctrine, which goes back to Judaism, is echoed in the Greek translation of Deuteronomy 32:8. "When the Most High divided the nations, when he separated the sons of Adam, he appointed the bounds of people according to the number of the angels of God." The Book of Daniel speaks of the angels of Greece and Persia (Dan. 10:13-21). The Jewish apocalypses were familiar with this doctrine, [1] as was Philo of Alexandria. [2] The New Testament seems to presuppose it in Acts 17:26.[3] "And from one man he has created the whole human race and made them live all over the face of the earth, determining their appointed times and the boundaries of their lands." It is found again in the Fathers. Irenaeus makes mention of it, [4] and Clement of Alexandria writes: "The presiding powers of the angels have been distributed according to the nations and the cities." [5] And elsewhere, "The angels have been apportioned among the nations according to an ancient and divine decree." [6] Hippolytus says the same thing.[7]

[1] *Hen.,* 89, 59.   [2] *De post. Cain,* 26.
[3] See O. Cullmann, *Christus und die Zeit,* 169-186.
[4] *Adv. haer.,* 3, 12, 9.   [5] *Strom.,* 6, 17.
[6] *Ibid.,* 7, 2.   [7] *Comm. in Dan.,* 4, 40, 4.

Origen accords this doctrine a place of importance in his system. [8] "Some certain spiritual powers," he writes, "have come into a presiding office over particular nations in this world." [9] In accordance with the Jewish tradition, he relates this division of the peoples under the angels to their dispersion after the tower of Babel. [10] The Fathers of the fourth century were also familiar with the angels of the nations. "That there are some angels set at the head of entire nations is the teaching of Moses when he speaks in his canticle [Deut. 32:8]," writes St. Basil. [11] "There are great numbers of archons and ethnarchs each of whom has been set up to protect and watch over the nation which is placed under his authority." [12] St. John Chrysostom gives the same testimony. [13] And Pseudo-Dionysius incorporates this teaching into his general exposition of angelology. "Theology has apportioned to the angels all things which pertain to us, naming Michael the angel of Israel . . . and giving other names to the angels of the other nations. In fact, the Most High has determined the boundaries of the nations according to the number of the angels of God." [14]

This mission of the angels to the nations is concerned first of all with protection and temporal assistance. Origen, following the Jewish tradition, attributes to them a part in the origin of the various languages.[15] But their mission is primarily spiritual. In that respect, according to certain authors,

[8] J. Danielou, *Origène*, pp. 222-235.
[9] *De prin.*, 3, 3, 3.
[10] *Contra Cels.*, 5, 30.
[11] *Adv. Eun.*, 3, 1.
[12] *Comm. in Is.*, 10, 240.
[13] *De laud. Paul.*, 2. See also St. Hilary, *Tract. Ps.* 61 and 67.
[14] *Hier. coel.*, 9, 2.
[15] *Contra Cels.*, 5, 30. See J. Danielou, *Les sources juives de la doctrine des anges des nations chez Origène. Rech. Sc. Relig.* 1951, p. 132.

they play a role in the natural revelation of God. As Pseudo-Dionysius puts it, "The angels entrusted with the sacred care of each nation lifted up all those who wanted to follow them toward the one single universal principle." [16] It is their mission to lead the pagan peoples to God. This is a very fertile doctrine from the missionary point of view. The heathens are not entirely deprived of aid: the angels of God assist them, trying to lead them to the true God, preparing the way of the Lord. Origen sees one of these angels in the Macedonian who appeared to St. Paul to beg aid of him.[17]

This is also important for judging the pagan religions. No matter how perverted they are, they retain some vestige of the natural revelation, and that vestige is due to the angels who have passed it on to them and who strive to keep it alive among them. Clement, whose favorable attitude regarding the values of the pagan authors is well known, does not hesitate to compare the role of the angels in the communication of the Law to the Jews to their role in delivering philosophy to the Greeks. "The divine power procures all manner of visible goods for us through the angels. This method of operation is manifest in the covenants of the Jews, the legislation of the Greeks, and the teachings of philosophy." [18] And he connects this directly with the doc-

[16] *Hier. coel.*, 9, 3.   [17] *Hom. in Luc.*, 12.

[18] *Strom.*, 6, 17. The bond between the angels and philosophy is fixed in St. Paul (1 Cor. 2:6). L. Cerfaux writes: "The powers came in between: philosophy was theirs. The angels who have given the Law and the powers both act in the same sense" (*Op. cit.*, pp. 191 and 199). But Cerfaux is wrong in saying: "The early writers (Origen) interpreted the archontes as evil Powers" (*ibid.*, p. 199). Actually, this word, in St. Paul as in Origen, is always ambiguous. If St. Paul insists upon the perversion that the evil angels have brought to bear upon philosophy, this does not exclude the possibility of good angels having had a part to play in its communication.

trine of the angels of the nations: "God gave philosophy to the Greeks by means of the lower angels. In fact, in accordance with a divine and ancient order, the nations have been distributed among the angels." [19]

Thus, for certain of the early Fathers, whatever part of truth was known to the pagan peoples and was later to be recognized and taken up by Christianity, the wisdom of Roman law, the philosophical truths arrived at by Plato and Aristotle—all this came to them from the providence of the one God acting through the ministry of the angels. "The universal providence of the One Most High God has, for the salvation of all the nations, entrusted them to angels who are to lead them toward God." [20] This means all nations. Not only the partial truths arrived at by the Greeks and the Romans, but also those of other peoples, have been communicated through the medium of angels and are capable of being incorporated into Christianity. Origen declares that this applies to the "secret and occult philosophy of the Egyptians and the astrology of the Chaldeans," and even "the Hindu claims pertaining to the science of the Most High God." [21] It is remarkable to hear Origen declare that the wisdom of India contains elements of truth which Christianity can recognize. Now, this truth has come to each of these nations through their angels. "We read in Scripture," continues Origen, "that there are princes over each nation—and the context makes it quite clear that they are angels and not men. It is these princes and the other powers of this world who each have a separate science and a special doctrine to teach." [22]

Origen's allusion to the astral religion of the Chaldeans

[19] *Strom.*, 7, 2.
[20] *Hier. coel.*, 9, 4.
[21] *De princ.*, 3, 3, 2.
[22] *Ibid.*

is also noteworthy. He returns to this point again: "[The astral religion] was given by God to all the peoples who are under heaven, except to those whom He wished to set aside for Himself as His chosen part." [23] This statement might seem to be a justification of the cult given to the stars themselves; but it can be interpreted in a different way, as referring to the knowledge of the existence of God which is obtained by means of the world covenant, and by means of His providence as revealed particularly through the contemplation of the star-filled heavens. [24]

It is in this sense in particular that the Fathers of the Church have interpreted the religion of Abraham before his conversion. He was a "Chaldean"; that is to say, in their opinion, he adored the true God as he beheld Him present in the "star-filled heavens." [25] It is worthy of note that the Encyclical *Evangelii Praecones*, in giving an example of the authentic values encountered in pagan religions, cites a text of St. Basil which alludes to "the Chaldeism of Daniel."

It seems that Eusebius, too, might well have been an authoritative exegete of Origen's thought when he explained his doctrine by relating it to the Epistle to the Romans. "God has apportioned all the nations (except the Jews, whom He reserved for Himself) to invisible rulers, the angels, in accord with a most mysterious plan. These angels, rulers and shepherds, judged it well that the men who were not able to contemplate the invisible in spirit, nor raise themselves to such a degree because of their weakness, should turn toward realities which they saw in the heavens,

[23] *Contra Cels.*, 5, 10.
[24] On this question see A. J. Festugière, *Le dieu cosmique*, pp. 120-250.
[25] Gregory of Nyssa, *Contra Eun.*, 12; Justin, *Dial.*, 55, 1 and 121, 2. Cf. Deut. 4:19; 29:21; Clement of Alexandria, *Strom.*, 4, 14.

the sun, the moon, and the stars. These objects, in fact, which hold a place of eminence in the visible universe, drew the eyes of those who saw them upward as close as possible to the King of the universe, into His antechamber, so to speak, and by their grandeur and beauty led them to contemplate, by analogy, the Creator of the universe. For, says the divine apostle, since the creation of the world the realities of God have been seen by means of created things." [26]

This is the relationship which Eusebius sees between the astral religion and the text of the Epistle to the Romans. For him there is no question of adoring the stars, or the cosmos itself, but rather of recognizing God the Creator through the movements of the heavens. That was precisely the plan of the natural revelation, and it is seen in reference to the angels with whom St. Paul connected the revelation of Sinai. The sun and the stars appeared as a sacred symbol of the divine, as natural sacraments. This is explained by Lactantius, a contemporary of Eusebius: "God kindled the sun, the unparalleled and sparkling source of light, as evidence of His unparalleled majesty." [27] Prudentius echoes the same doctrine: "God has placed before our eyes a remarkable symbol of His unity. Throughout the immense arena of the heavens there is but one single flame which marks the revolution of days, one single sun which weaves the web of the year." [28]

Thus the angels were charged with leading the nations toward the one true God. But, as a matter of fact, the study of religions does not show that they succeeded especially well. Though containing bits of the truth, all the religions of the world before Christ, except Judaism, are profoundly corrupt. Why? Pseudo-Dionysius answers: "If anyone asks,

[26] *Dem. Ev.*, 4, 7-8.
[27] *Inst. div.*, 2, 5.
[28] *Hamartigenes*, 67-71.

'How does it happen that the Jewish people was elevated to
the splendor of a theocracy?' we must answer that the angels
fulfilled their office of guardians with perfect honesty, and
that it is not their fault if the other nations went astray into
the cult of false gods. For it was these nations themselves,
of their own impulse, which abandoned the right way of
spiritual ascent toward the divine. Their foolish worship of
things which they thought possessed a certain divinity clearly
shows their egoism and their presumption." [29] Pseudo-Dionysius takes up here, in relation to the angels of the nations,
the same doctrine that St. Paul expresses in the Epistle to
the Romans 1:23. "God has made Himself known to the
nations by means of the visible realities of the world," but
men "have changed the glory of the incorruptible God for
an image made like to corruptible man and to birds and
four-footed beasts and creeping things."

The traces of truth were everywhere profoundly corrupted
by idolatry. Only where they found souls entirely open to
the light of God were the angels able to accomplish their
mission and lead them to the knowledge of the true God by
means of the revelation of the cosmos. There is one outstanding example of these exceptions, Melchisedech. Pseudo-
Dionysius reports of him: "The angels entrusted with the
sacred care of each nation lifted up all those who wanted to
follow them faithfully. A witness of this is Melchisedech,
King of Salem in the time of Abraham, from the Gentiles
and in the midst of the Gentiles, but a priest most pleasing
to God. For Sacred Scripture is not content to represent
Melchisedech as a friend of God; it also calls him a priest of
the one true God, to indicate to all that his role was not only
to be personally converted to God, but also to lead others
along the way of spiritual ascent." [30] And already Justin

[29] *Hier. coel.*, 9, 3.
[30] *Ibid.*

ranked Socrates, Job, and Plato among the disciples of the Word, before His coming.

For Pseudo-Dionysius the greatest obstacle to the activity of the angels was the evil will of men. But a second must be added to it—the activity of the demons. If the nations have their good angels sent by God to assist and guide them, they are also the prey of demons who try to turn them away from the true God. The favorite method employed is to enmesh them in idolatry. This idolatry, in which St. Paul saw the corruption of the religion handed down to the nations by God, is essentially the work of the devil. Thus the demons take the place of the angels in the government and direction of nations, and thus there is question of evil angels more frequently than of good angels among them.

This origin of idolatry is described by all the Fathers. The Jewish apocalypses attributed it to the demons.[31] Eusebius cites Romans 1:21-23, in this regard, where the corruption of natural religion into idolatry is marked out. This was not what had been from the beginning. "In earlier times men turned only toward the stars of heaven and knew nothing of idols and the illusions of the devil. That is what I have established in the *Preparation to the Gospel*, where I demonstrated that the earliest men did not fashion idols and did not serve invisible demons, but only those spirits among whom Scripture tells us the nations were apportioned. And it is time that the Greeks recognize the fact that, upon the evidence of their own texts, idolatry and the cult of the demons are a recent superstition, unknown in the religion of the ancients." [32]

This explanation of Eusebius is interesting in that it helps

[31] *Hen.*, 19, 1; 99, 7.
[32] *Dem. Ev.*, 4, 9. See Clement of Alexandria, *Protrept.*, 44, 1, 3. For Methodius, mankind before the deluge was still living "in the familiarity of the angels" (*Conv.*, 7, 5).

resolve the ambiguity which arises from seeing the angels of the nations appear now as good, now as evil spirits. [33] In reality, there are both kinds. God entrusted the nations to good angels who taught them the religion of the true God as He makes Himself known in the movement of the heavens, but the evil angels turned them away from the natural religion and caught them in a net of perversion and idolatry. This explanation corresponds closely to the religious history of the pagan peoples as described in the Epistle to the Romans. Eusebius here sketches a whole theology of the history of religions by distinguishing, among the non-Biblical religions, first a cosmic revelation, which is that of the true God; and then idolatry, which is the perversion of it.

[33] See L. Cerfaux, *op. cit.*, pp. 77-83; J. Danielou, *Origène*, p. 227.

3

The Angels of the Nativity

The coming of Christ would seem, according to St. Paul, to have necessarily put an end to the ministry of the angels. It is Jesus who is the sole minister of the New Covenant.[1] But actually this is not so. Christ is indeed the center of the history of salvation, but the whole world of angels is round about to serve Him. On the one hand, the angels who were entrusted with the care of earthly affairs receive Him with joy and place themselves at His service; and on the other hand, the angels of heaven come down with Him to be the ministers and witnesses of His work. The hierarchi-

[1] "The Lord Himself is the Shepherd of those who have not been converted, not only through the angels, but by His own activity" (Eusebius, *Dem. Ev.*, 7, 2).

cal point of view is visible here within the range of the historical. This manifestation of the angels fills especially two moments in the life of Christ: its beginning and its end, the infancy and the glory, the Nativity and the Ascension. It is in connection with these two mysteries that the angels are particularly signaled out in the Gospel.

The Fathers of the Church present the ages which preceded Christ as marking an increase in the power of the demons. The vestiges of a monotheistic revelation, communicated to all men through the ministry of the angels, grow faint with the flourishing of idolatry and devil worship. Even in the one part of the world which God reserved for Himself, the people of Israel, the rising tide of sin continues to mount. The angels to whom the nations were entrusted are powerless to stem the flood of evil. "Before the birth of Christ these angels could be of little use to those entrusted to them and their attempts were not followed by success. . . . Whenever the Angel of the Egyptians helped the Egyptians, there was hardly a single proselyte who believed in God." [2]

St. John Chrysostom says the same thing: "God set all things in motion through the angels, and nothing was working out well." [3] Eusebius develops this pessimistic view with greater preciseness. "In such a flood of evil, since the angels who had first been set in charge of the nations could do nothing for their subjects and were able only to look after the rest of creation—being set up over those parts of the world and following absolutely the will of God, the Architect of all things, and yet unable to help stay the fall of mankind because of man's own free choice of evil—then a grave and all but incurable disease laid hold of all upon earth. The peoples, each in its own way, were driven on by evil spirits and fell into a frightful abyss of vices. . . . Even

[2] Origen, *Hom. in Luc.*, 12.   [3] *Hom. in Eph.*, 1.

the Jewish nation was drawn into their corruption." [4] For
Eusebius the angels, discouraged at their lack of success
among the pagan peoples, have to be satisfied with the administration of the visible world.

But in the midst of this desperate situation the Word of
God becomes incarnate, in order to come to the aid of His
angels. Eusebius continues as follows: "Now, since such
great evils had fallen upon the whole of the inhabited earth
through the wicked spirits and their leader, since none of
the angels was able to prevent these evils, and since the race
He loved was wallowing in the depths of iniquity, it was
most fitting that the Word of God, the Saviour of all,
through the merciful will of the Father's love for men,
should at first send forth short and feeble rays of His own
bright light through His Prophet Moses and the other God-
like men who went before him. But since none who came
after could bring a remedy against the evils and the activity
of the demons continued to increase day by day, the Saviour
Himself came to men as their Physician and helped His
angels in their work for the salvation of men." [5]

That is why the angels in charge of the nations welcomed
the coming of the Saviour with great happiness. "The
Saviour places under His powerful protection no longer only
Israel, just and God-minded, nor His own portion, but all
the nations of earth who were first apportioned to the many
angels and became involved in all manner of ungodliness;
to all of them He announces the knowledge and friendship
that is to be found in His Father, God . . . When He was
seen by His own angels, who were first set up over the nations, they immediately recognized their Lord coming to
their aid and went to Him joyously, to minister to Him.

[4] *Dem. Ev.*, 4, 10. See also Hilary, *Tract. Ps.* 52; Eusebius,
Theoph., PG 24, 629 BC.
[5] *Ibid.*

Just as Sacred Scripture says in the Gospel, 'The angels drew near and ministered to Him.' And elsewhere: 'There was a multitude of the heavenly host praising God and saying: Glory to God in the highest and on earth peace, good will to men.' " [6]

The mystery of the Christmas angels is primarily that of the angels of the nations surrounding the Infant God who has come to the aid of the pagan peoples entrusted to them, for whom they put forth all their labor in vain. [7] But it is not merely that. It is also the mystery of the hosts of angels who descend from heaven with the Word as He becomes incarnate, to surround Him with their adoration and to serve Him as the Lord. St. Hilary gathers the Scriptural references to this truth when he writes: "When [Christ] comes down to assume humanity, a heavenly entourage accompanies Him. When Mary receives the good tidings, when the shepherds see the heavenly assembly and hear their voices, when the devil tempts Him, the angels minister to Him. For, although He came entirely in the form of a slave, nonetheless He acted in the strength of His Father's majesty, and that is why the heavens bow down when the Power and Honor of the heavenly beings (that is, the Son of God) comes down to earth." [8]

---

[6] *Dem. Ev.*, 4, 10. See *Comm. in Ps. 71.*

[7] See Origen: "The coming of Christ into the world was a great joy for those to whom the care of men and nations had been entrusted" (*Hom. in Luc.*, 12). Later Hilary, *Comm. in Matt.*, 7, 3; *Tract. Ps. 2.* This seems to be in harmony with the thought of St. Paul on the good angels. L. Cerfaux sums it up as follows: "They preserved intact their first appointment to the government of creation (quite different from the evil angels) and have for their mission the duty of leading creation to God by becoming perfectly and spontaneously subject to the Kingdom of Christ" (*op. cit.*, p. 83).

[8] *Tract. Ps. 143.* See *Dem. Ev.*, 6, 18; 6, 25; 10, 7.

Origen has already shown the angels eager to descend with the Word. "When the angels saw the Prince of the heavenly host tarrying among the places of earth, they entered by the way that He had opened, following their Lord and obeying the will of Him who apportioned to their guardianship those who believe in Him. The angels are in the service of your salvation. If He descended into a body, they have been granted to the Son of God to follow Him. They say among themselves, 'If He has put on mortal flesh, how can we remain doing nothing? Come, angels, let us all descend from heaven.' That is why there was a multitude of the heavenly host praising and glorifying God when Christ was born. Everything is filled with angels." [9]

Thus Origen interprets Luke's text, not as referring to the angels of the nations, but rather to the heavenly hosts who have come down with Christ. Both of these interpretations will be clarified later. For now it will only be noted that the angels of heaven appeared as the ministers and servants of Christ in the accomplishment of His work.[10] Gregory Nazianzen calls them "the initiated of the incarnation." For it is to them that the mystery, hidden in God from all eternity, has been revealed for the first time. "Gabriel could not have known of the mysteries except through the Holy Spirit," writes St. Basil. [11] And it was revealed to them first because they were to be its messengers. "Even in what concerns the divine mysteries of the love of Jesus for men it is the angels who were first initiated." [12]

Even with the coming of Christ, then, the angels remain the messengers of the divine revelations. Pseudo-Dionysius

[9] Hom. in Ez., 1, 7.
[10] Cyril of Jerusalem, PG 33, 673 B.
[11] PG 31, 37.
[12] Pseudo-Dionysius, Hier. coel., 4, 4. This remains the common teaching. See St. Thomas, ST, 1, 57, 5.

insists upon this point. "It is through their mediation that the grace of the knowledge of the mystery of Christ comes down even to us. So the most divine Gabriel revealed to the high priest Zachary that the child to be born to him beyond all expectation by the grace of God would be the announcer of the work of the Man-God Jesus. It is likewise Gabriel who revealed to Mary that the inexpressible mystery of God's holy incarnation would be accomplished in her. Another angel informed Joseph of the full and complete accomplishment of the divine promises made to his forbear David. Still another announced the good news to the shepherds at the very time that the whole heavenly host passed on to the inhabitants of earth their renowned canticle of God's glory." [13]

Not only are the angels the messengers of the mystery of Christ among men, but as Pseudo-Dionysius profoundly remarks, they also have to fill the role of messengers toward the humanity of Christ. "Let us lift up our eyes to the highest revelations of Scripture. I note first of all that Jesus Himself, the super-essential cause of every essence that dwells below heaven, having condescended to take on human nature without the slightest change of His own nature, in no way abandoned the order He had established, but submitted Himself with docility to the forms handed down through the angels from the Father. It was also through their mediation that the Father's decree concerning the flight into Egypt was made known to Joseph. And it is through this same mediation of the angels that I see Jesus submitting Himself to the decrees of the Father." [14]

The ministry of the angels toward the humanity of the Word extends from His nativity to His agony. But there is one mystery in which the angels can be of no assistance—the descent into hell. Only the Lord of the angels can

[13] *Ibid.*   [14] *Ibid.*

descend into the domain of death to destroy the power of death. That is what Eusebius explains in his commentary on the Psalm verse "For tribulation is very near, for there is none to help me" (21:12): "The bitterest of the sufferings heaped upon Him then was that not one of the angels who were propitious and eager to be of aid, nor any of the divine Powers, dared set foot in the domain of death or work with Him to relieve the souls present there. He alone could actually go on without fear, since it was only for Him that the gates of death had opened, and the prison guards of death were terrified at seeing Him advance alone. It was upon seeing the impious domination of this tyrant, so strong that none of the Powers of heaven would dare take their place beside Christ in the lower regions and work with Him for the salvation of the souls there, that He says with good reason that the final agony is near at hand and there is no one to assist Him." [15]

Pseudo-Dionysius obviously likes to emphasize the permanence of the angels' mediation after the coming of Jesus. The older Fathers, on the contrary, after St. Paul, stressed the passing of this mediation. Actually, these are merely two aspects of one mystery. On the one hand, it is true that the older economy was transmitted much more directly through the ministry of angels and that this mediation ceased with Christ, who is Himself the "Angel" of the New Covenant. That, since he minimizes the history of salvation, Pseudo-Dionysius failed to recognize. But, on the other hand, it is also true that, even though the angels no longer play the role of mediator, they remain the ministers of Him who is the sole Mediator, and consequently their ministry continues after the coming of Christ.

It must be added, however, that this ministry appears much more subordinate now than it did to Dionysius.

[15] *Dem. Ev.*, 10.

Man now has in Christ immediate access to the Father without passing through the intermediary of the angels, who are
only there to aid him in the first stages of his ascent. Finally
the angels of the higher hierarchies who come down with
the Word, since they surround Him with their perpetual
adoration, are His messengers not only among men but also
among the lower angels who are more immediately charged
with the government of earthly things. Pseudo-Dionysius
makes this view the central point of his angelology. "The
higher order, which is composed of the Cherubim, the Seraphim and the Thrones and which is closest of all, by reason
of its dignity, to the secret sanctuary, mysteriously initiates
the second order, composed of Dominations, Virtues, and
Powers. This order, in its turn, reveals the mysteries to the
Principalities, the Archangels, and the Angels, who are set
in charge of the human hierarchies." [16] It is a well-known
fact that St. Thomas takes up this doctrine and integrates
it with the common tradition.

The case under consideration is an example of the illumination of lower orders by higher ones. This theme of an an-
nunciation to the angels appeared in Origen. He interprets
the shepherds of Bethlehem allegorically as the angels of the
nations, making a play on the word shepherd, which applies
to the one as well as to the other. "The shepherds can be
considered as the angels to whom men are entrusted. They
all had need of assistance so that the nations in their charge
would be well governed. It is to them that the angel came to
announce the birth of the true Shepherd." [17] This is the
same theme of the expectation of the angels, charged with
the care of things on earth and powerless to lead them to
good. They were waiting for a divine intervention to come
to their assistance. That is why the heavenly messengers
turned to them first of all to announce the good news.

[16] *Hier. coel.*, 9, 2.   [17] *Hom. in Luc.*, 12.

Gregory of Nyssa develops the same idea, in regard to Psalm 23, in his *Sermon on the Ascension:* "The most high Prophet, having departed from within himself, to the extent that he is no longer bound by the weight of the body, and joining the company of the Powers above this world, reveals their words to us when, as they escort the Lord in His descent, they order the angels who surround the earth, to whom the care of human life has been confided, to lift up their gates. *Tollite portas, principes, vestras, et elevamini, portae eternales, et introibit rex gloriae.* And since He who contains all within Himself accommodates Himself to the level of those who receive Him, He not only becomes a man among men, but, coming as He does to the angels, He condescends to their nature as well. Thus, the gate-keepers ask the Prophet, *Quis est iste rex gloriae?* And they answer that He is strong and mighty in battle and that He is to enter into combat with him who made humanity captive and destroy him who held the power of death." [18]

We can ignore Christ's assumption of the form of an angel in passing through the circle of the angels. [19] This view, which goes back to the *Ascension of Isaias,* rests on speculations which need not be gone into. [20] But what *is* interesting for us is that which concerns the two categories of angels. On the one hand, the powers that are above the sensible world escort the Lord in His descent, preparing His path for Him; and on the other hand, the angels to whom is entrusted the care of human affairs are like porters who are to verify the identity of those who enter. That is why, in the

[18] *Serm. asc.,* PG 46, 693 A.
[19] See J. Barbel, *Christos Angelos,* pp. 297-311.
[20] St. Thomas retains what is true in this teaching by speaking of an assumption of men according to degrees of grace corresponding to that of the angels, without any transformation of natures. Cf. ch. 9.

one mystery of Christ's descent, we find the two lines of theological thought which we saw at the outset in the angels of the Nativity: there is the ascending line of the angels of the nations, which stems from Origen, and the descending line of the angels of heaven, which is connected with the Gospel. Thus it becomes a synthesis of the angelology of the Nativity.

This joy of the nations is all the greater since the revelation of Christ infinitely surpasses their expectations. They did, indeed, hope to see the peoples entrusted to them liberated from the yoke of idolatry, but they did not even conceive of their being called to be the sons of God. Chrysostom, commenting on Ephesians 3, where the call of the nations is revealed to the angels, writes the following: "St. Paul speaks here of a mystery, because not even the angels knew it. The angels only knew that the Lord had chosen His people as His portion (Deut. 32:8) and that 'the Prince of Persia is set against me' (Dan. 10:13). That is why we need not be surprised that they did not know this, since, properly speaking, it is the Gospel. God had said He would save His people Israel, but had said nothing about the nations. The angels knew that the nations were called, but could not imagine that they would be called to the same end and would be seated upon the throne of God." [21]

But this final thought, far beyond the mystery of the Nativity, brings us to the Ascension.

[21] *Hom. in Eph.*, 3.

4

The Angels of the Ascension

If the mystery of the Nativity inaugurates the work of Christ, that of the Ascension completes it. Just as the angels were entrusted with the secrets of the first, they are the open admirers of the second, after having assisted Christ throughout the interval which separated these two events, from the temptation to the Resurrection. Gregory Nazianzen shows Christ entering into heaven, after having recovered the lost drachma and "calling together the friendly powers to share His joy with them just as He initiated them to His incarnation." [1] And Chrysostom, speaking of the Ascension, compares the participation of the angels in the two mysteries:

[1] Or., 38, 14.

"When our Lord was born according to the flesh, the angels, seeing that He was being reconciled with man, cried 'Glory to God in the highest.' Do you want to know how they rejoiced in the Ascension? Listen to the account in the Bible, 'They rise and descend continuously.' That is the behavior of those who want to contemplate a very special sight. They want to see the unheard-of spectacle of man appearing in heaven. That is why the angels are constantly showing themselves: when He is born, when He dies, when He rises into heaven." [2]

This text of Chrysostom makes two points clear. First of all, the angels are present at the Ascension. This is asserted in the Acts of the Apostles (1:10): "Two men stood by them in white garments." And Cyril of Jerusalem writes that "the angels assisted Him in His ascent." [3] Though the Acts speak only of the presence of the angels, tradition shows them accompanying Christ in His ascent. Sometimes they even carry Him triumphantly upon their shoulders. This sort of picture is found particularly in the early popular writings, such as the *Ascension of Isaias* and the *Gospel of Peter*, [4] and again in sculptured tombs of the Middle Ages. [5] Sometimes the angels form a triumphant escort. This is how Eusebius describes the Ascension: "The Virtues of heaven, seeing Him begin to rise, surrounded Him to form His escort, proclaiming His Ascension as they cried, 'Rise up, gates everlasting, and the King of Glory will enter.' These things were accomplished in what the Acts record for us, 'And when he had said these things, he was lifted up before their eyes' (1:9)." [6]

[2] *Serm. asc.*, 4. See also Gregory of Nyssa, *Serm. asc.*, PG 46, 693.
[3] *Catech.*, 4, 13.   [4] *Asc. Is.*, 3, 15; *Ev. Petr.*, 40-43.
[5] See F. J. Doelger, *Sol salutis*, 2nd ed., pp. 212 f.
[6] *Comm. in Ps.* 17.

Psalm 23, quoted here, was applied to the Ascension early and has contributed much to forming this representation. Elsewhere Eusebius cites Psalm 46: "It was fitting that the angels who had served Him during His life on earth should precede the Son of God in His Ascension into heaven, flinging wide the gates of heaven and breaking forth into the angelic words which the Psalmist calls jubilation and sound of triumph: 'God is ascended with jubilee, and the Lord with the sound of trumpet.' " [7]

But there is more. The relation of the angels of the Ascension has a much deeper meaning. [8] It is bound up with substance of the mystery. The Ascension is not only the elevation of Christ in His Body into the midst of the angels; to be more theologically precise, it is the exaltation of human nature, which the Word of God has united to Himself, above all the angelic orders which are superior to it. This is a complete reversal of the regular order, and it affords the angels an "unheard-of" spectacle.

This theology of the ascension was developed by St. Paul in the captivity epistles. The Epistle to the Ephesians tells us that God "is manifesting his mighty power, which he has wrought in Christ, in raising him from the dead, and setting him at his right hand in heaven above every Principality and Power and Virtue and Domination—in short, above every name that is named, not only in this world, but also in that which is to come. And all things he made subject under his feet" (1:20-22). The point is, then, that the Word Incarnate is established king over all of creation. St. Paul allows his readers to surmise that the angelic forces are more numerous than is generally thought. Thus, to the wonderment of the heavenly forces, the human nature is exalted

[7] *Comm. in Ps. 23.* See Hilary, *Tract. Ps. 67.*
[8] See H. Bietenhard, *op. cit.,* p. 67.

in the Person of Christ, above every angelic nature, known
or unknown.

St. Paul returns to this same idea elsewhere: "Therefore
God also has exalted him and given him the name that is
above every name, so that at the name of Jesus every knee
should bend of those in heaven, on earth, and under the
earth, and every tongue should confess that Jesus Christ is
Lord, to the glory of God the Father" (Phil. 2:9-11).

It is at the Name of Jesus—that is, Christ made Man—
that every knee is to bend in heaven. The overwhelming
revelation made to the angels in the mystery of the Ascension is not that they are to adore the eternal Word—that
is already the object of their liturgy; but rather that they
are to adore the Word Incarnate—and that overturns all of
heaven, just as the Incarnation revolutionized all of earth.[9]

St. Chrysostom develops the thought of St. Paul when he
writes: "Today we are raised up into heaven, we who seemed
unworthy even of earth. We are exalted above the heavens;
we arrive at the kingly throne. The nature which caused
the Cherubim to keep guard over Paradise is seated today
above the Cherubim. Was it not enough to be elevated
above the heavens? Was it not enough to have place among
the angels? Was not such a glory beyond all expression? But
He rose above the angels, He passed the Cherubim, He
went higher than the Seraphim, He bypassed the Thrones,
He did not stop until He arrived at the very Throne of
God." [10] This is really a commentary on the following text
from the Epistle to the Hebrews: "He has taken his seat at
the right hand of the Majesty on high, having become so
much superior to the angels as he has inherited a more ex-
cellent name than they" (1:3-4).

If the mystery of the Nativity is also that of the revelation made by the angels of heaven to those of earth, then

[9] See also Hebrews 1:5; 2:13.   [10] *Serm. asc.,* 3.

the mystery of the Ascension is the mystery of the revelation made by the angels of earth to the angels of heaven. Just as, at the Nativity, we see the Word descend, surrounded by the angels of heaven, and meet the guardian angels of earth, so now we see Him rise, accompanied by the angels of earth, and meet the angels who guard the gates of heaven. But these do not recognize Him, because He appears united to the human nature which He assumed and bearing the marks of His passion. Thus they question the angels who are accompanying Him to find out who He is. This is a traditional theme, resting principally upon two Biblical texts, Psalm 23:7-10, which has already been seen, and Isaias 63:1, "Who is this that cometh from Edom, with dyed garments from Bosra?" [11]

Justin describes the scene. "Lift up your gates, rulers; be lifted up, ye everlasting gates, and the King of Glory will enter. Who is this King of Glory? It, is the Lord, mighty and powerful in battle. Lift up your gates, rulers; be lifted up, ye gates of eternity, and the King of Glory will enter. Who is this King of Glory? The Lord of the Powers, He is the King of Glory. Now, I have already proved that the Lord of the Powers is not Solomon, but rather our Christ after He had risen from the dead and was on His way to heaven. The rulers established by God in the heavens are called upon to open the gates of the heavens so that He that is the King of Glory may enter and rise to His seat at the right hand of the Father, until He makes His enemies the footstool of His feet—as has been made clear by the other psalm. But when the rulers in heaven saw Him without beauty and honor in His appearance and deprived of glory, they failed to recognize Him and demanded, 'Who is this King of Glory?' " [12]

[11] See J. Danielou, *Bible et liturgie*, pp. 409-428.
[12] *Dial.*, 36, 4-5.

The application of this psalm to the Ascension is anterior to Justin. It goes back to Apostolic times and can already be found in the *Apocalypse of Peter*. [13] But Justin is the first to develop the dialogue between the angels of heaven who do not recognize the Word made Flesh and the angels of earth who reveal His identity.

This commentary is to be found throughout the whole of early tradition. Irenaeus has it: "David says somewhere that He was to be lifted up into heaven. 'Princes, raise up your gates; rise up, gates of eternity, and the King of Glory shall pass through.' The gates of eternity are heaven. Made invisible through His Incarnation, He has risen up to heaven. Seeing Him approach, the lower angels cried out to those who were above them, 'Open your gates; rise up, ye gates of eternity; the King of Glory will enter.' And when the angels from above asked in their astonishment, 'Who is He?' those who saw Him cried out anew, 'It is the Lord, strong and mighty. It is the King of Glory.'" [14] Irenaeus paints a fine picture of Christ ascending among the wondering hierarchies of the angels. This is well in accord with the deep meaning of the theological mystery of the Ascension, which is the exaltation of the humanity that Christ united to Himself above all the orders of angels (Eph. 1: 18-22).

Athanasius presents the same tradition. But it must be noted that, for him, the angels who accompany Christ in His ascent are not the angels of the earth, but those who had descended with Him. "The angels of the Lord who followed Him upon earth, seeing Him arise, announced His coming to the Virtues of heaven, so that they might open their gates. The Powers were filled with amazement at seeing Him in the flesh. That is why they cried, 'Who is this?'

[13] *Rev. Or. Chrét.*, 1910, p. 317.
[14] *Dem.*, 84.

astounded by this mysterious order of salvation. And the
Angels rising with Christ answered them, 'The Lord of
Powers, He is the King of Glory who teaches the great
mystery to those who are in heaven: that the King of Glory
has won the victory over the spiritual enemy.' " [15] The entry
of the Incarnate Word into·heaven appears much like an
unforeseen revelation made to the heavenly powers.

With Origen appears the text of Isaias 63, and the allusion to the blood of the Passion. "When He came forward
the Victor, His Body raised up from the dead, certain of the
Powers said, 'Who is this that comes from Bosra, with His
garments dyed red?' But those who were escorting Him
said to those in charge of the gates of heaven, 'Open, ye
gates of eternity.' " [16] This feature is repeated in Gregory
of Nyssa. After having described the angels of the earth who
did not recognize Christ in His descent, this time, con-
versely, he shows that "our guardians form an escort and
order the Powers who are above the world to open, so that
He may be adored among them once again. But they do
not recognize Him because he has put on the poor tunic
of our nature and because His garments were dyed crimson
in the winepress of human evils. This time it is they who
cry, 'Who is this King of Glory?' " [17] Likewise Ambrose:
"Even the angels doubted when Christ arose, seeing Him
rising into heaven in the flesh. They said, 'Who is this King
of Glory?' and while some of them were saying, 'Lift up
your gates, princes, and the King of Glory will enter,' others
were doubting and saying. 'Who is this that comes up from
Edom?' " [18]

St. Gregory Nazianzen gathers together the whole of this

[15] *Exp. in Ps.* 23.
[16] *Comm. in Jo.*, 6, 56.
[17] PG 46, 693 G.
[18] *De myst.*, 36.

tradition when he writes, "Join with the angels who escort and receive Him. Command the gates to be lifted still higher to receive Him who has grown to a great stature in His Passion. Answer those who doubt because of His Body and the marks of His suffering which He did not have when He descended, and who therefore ask, 'Who is this King of Glory?' Tell them that it is the Lord, powerful and strong in everything He has ever done and now does, both in His present struggles and in the trophy He will carry off for mankind. Give a double answer to their double question; and if they marvel and say, in the dramatic words of Isaias, 'Who is this that comes up from Edom and the regions of earth? How is it that He has neither blood nor body and yet His garments are stained red as the treader of grapes who has trodden out a winepress full of vintage?' then show them the beautiful tunic of the Body which suffered, and how it has grown even more beautiful in His Passion and been made to reflect the shining glory of the Godhead, so that He has no equal in beauty and attractiveness." [19]

Thus the mystery of the Ascension completely amazes the angels of heaven. For what it reveals to them is really a mystery, hidden up to then, an entirely new reality, disconcerting at first glance. The cosmological presentation of the descent and ascent must not deceive us. The true mystery of the Nativity is the self-abasement of the divine Person of the Word, a "little lower than the angels" (Hebrews 2:7). And the true mystery of the Ascension is the exaltation of human nature above all the worlds of the angels. That is the real double mystery which is dramatically represented by the descent and ascent in the midst of the choirs of angels. But this "dramaturgy," as St. Gregory Nazianzen calls it, must not conceal the reality it bears beneath it. It represents an overthrow of the natural order of things result-

[19] *Or.*, 45, 25.

ing from the revelation of a reality absolutely new and un-foreseeable. [20] That is why it throws the angels into a state of astonishment.

Gregory of Nyssa has admirably explained this revelation which the paradoxes of the Redemption of the Church made known to the angels: "Indeed it is through the Church that the great and manifold wisdom of God is made known to the Powers above the heavens, this wisdom which works great marvels by means of opposites. For life is produced by death, blessings by curses, glory by dishonor. In the past the heavenly powers were familiar with the simple and uniform wisdom of God, who worked marvels in conformity with His nature. But there was nothing different in what they saw, for the divine nature worked out all of creation by its power, producing beings by the mere impetus of His will, creating everything beautiful, fresh from the source of all beauty. Regarding the different aspect of divine wisdom which consists in the multiplication of opposites, they are now instructed by the Church, seeing the Word made flesh, life joined together with death, our wounds healed by His stripes, the strength of the adversary overcome by the weak-ness of the Cross, the invisible manifested in the flesh. All these works are different and no longer simple, and it is through the Church that the friends of the Bridegroom are taught about them and that their heart is touched, for they recognize in the mystery a new characteristic of the wisdom of God. And if I dare to express it thus, perhaps they saw

[20] This is based on Ephesians 3:10. The western tradition, after Augustine, holds that the mystery of the Incarnation was known to the angels from the beginning, whereas in the East it was maintained that the "mystery" was hidden to every creature. But no matter at what moment of time the "mystery" was revealed to the angels, it remains true that it is the revelation of a reality which was in itself new.

in the Bride the beauty of the Bridegroom, and learned to love Him who is invisible and incomprehensible to all. He whom no man has seen nor can see has made the Church His Body, forming it after His own image in such a way that by turning toward her the friends of the Bridegroom have learned to see the invisible more clearly in her." [21]

[21] *Hom. in Cant.*, 8.

The Angels and the Church

The angels of heaven hesitate at first, seeing the Incarnate Word ascend, before the paradox of human nature, the most lowly of all, exalted above all the choirs of heaven. But when the angels who are accompanying Christ have revealed the mystery to them, they exult with joy, for they have been waiting for this return of humanity into heaven, although they did not dream it would be so glorious. Their amazement gives way to joy. "Today," writes Chrysostom, "the angels have obtained what they were always waiting for; today the archangels have received what they ardently desired. They have seen our nature upon its royal throne, shining with immortal glory and beauty. Even though it has the honor of being exalted above them, they rejoice at our good, just as they suffered when we were deprived of it." [1]

I. THE ANGELS OF PARADISE

The words "even though it has the honor of being exalted above them" must be noted. They have their full meaning only if it is remembered that throughout an entire tradition the sin of the angels was explained as their refusal to recognize the dignity of Adam created in the image of God. This tradition appears particularly in the *Life of Adam and Eve.* The devil says to Adam, "O Adam, Michael had you come before the whole assembly of the angels and told them, 'Pay homage to the image of the Lord God as He has commanded.' And Michael was the first to pay homage to him and then he called me and said, 'Pay homage to the image of the God Jahweh.' And I answered, 'I will not pay homage to Adam.' And when Michael was about to force me to pay homage, I told him, 'I will not pay homage to someone who is lower than I am and who comes after me.' " [2]

The Fathers of the Church inherited this tradition. The first one in whose writings it appears is Athenagoras.[3] Irenaeus takes it up in the *Proof of the Apostolic Preaching,* where he says: "Great creations had been prepared in the world by God before man was created. A place had been given to man where he found himself provided with everything. In this place God, Creator of all things, had placed servants, each with his own particular office. A captain of a thousand men was in charge of this place and he was set at the head of his fellow soldiers. These soldiers were the angels, and the captain was an archangel . . . But he, see-

1 *Serm. asc.,* 4.
2 *Life of Adam and Eve,* 14.
3 *Suppl.,* 24.

ing the numerous favors that man had received from God, became envious of him and began to murmur. He brought about the ruin of man and made him a sinner by inducing him to violate the commandment of God with full malice. Thus the chief cause and instigator of sin was the angel through his trickery. He who had sinned against God was stricken and man was driven out of Paradise. And the angel, since he had followed his own inclinations in revolting and abandoning God, was called Satan in the Hebrew language, the same angel whom we call the devil." [4]

For Irenaeus, as for Athenagoras, it is the guardian angel of the earth who was jealous of man at his appearance and who caused man's fall at the same time as his own. This is found throughout an entire tradition which can be easily followed. Methodius of Philippi borrows the idea from Athenagoras and writes: "The spirit who was present about the earth, as Athenagoras has said, was created by God like the other angels and was charged with administering the substance of material natures. For this was the condition of the angels: they had been established by God to watch over the realities governed by Him, in such a way that it was God who watched over the whole of the universe by His providence, Himself holding all things within His power and directing the world infallibly, like a ship, through the rudder of His wisdom, and certain of the angels were set up to watch over each individual part of the universe. The others abode within the elements for which God had created and established them. But this one [Satan] grew proud and became perverted in the administration of the part entrusted to him; for he had become envious of our human lot." [5]

It is most likely from Methodius that Gregory of Nyssa inherited the tradition. "The intelligible world was in ex-

[4] *Dem. ap.*, 11-16.
[5] *De res.*, 1, 37.

istence before the other came to be, and each one of the
angelic powers received a certain portion of activity in the
administration of the universe from the one Authority which
directs all things. One of the Powers had been entrusted
with maintaining and governing the terrestrial sphere. Then
there was formed upon that earth a figure which represented
supreme power—the figure of man. In him resided the divine beauty of intelligible nature, joined with a secret vital
force. That is why the angel who had received as his portion the administration of the earth found it intolerable and
preposterous that from the nature which was set under his
authority there should arise a substance made to the image
and likeness of Beauty itself." [6]

Thus the sin of the angels was that they were jealous of
man. A whole theological tradition will retain this idea in
the form of a refusal on the part of Lucifer to accept the
future prospect of an Incarnation of the Word. Opposed
to this jealousy of the wicked angels toward the first Adam
is the friendliness of the good angels toward the new Adam.
In the scene of the temptation, after Christ has frustrated
the ruses of the Prince of this world, always jealous of man,
we see the angels approaching Christ to serve Him (Mark
1:23). And this seems to be an allusion to the new Adam. [7]

But it is above all else the Ascension which appears as
the counterpart of the fall. The jealousy of the angels had
caused the expulsion of man from Paradise; their rejoicing
greets the restoration of humanity in Paradise. The fall had

[6] *Dis. catech.*, 6, 5. This is also the teaching of John Damascene,
as quoted by St. Thomas: "The devil was one of the angelic
virtues set over earthly affairs." (PO 2, 4; PG 114, 873 D). See
also Prudentius, *Hamart.*, 184-205.

[7] See U. Holzmeister, "Jesus lebte mit den wilden Tieren," *Fest-
schrift Meinertz*, 1951, pp. 85-92. Ephrem seems to suppose
this teaching in fixing the fall of the devil on the sixth day. See
E. Beck, *Ephraems Hymnen ueber das Paradies*, 1951, p. 165.

broken the unity of the spiritual creation "by snatching man away from the company of the angels." [8] Since that time the angels were in waiting, hoping for the unity of the heavenly liturgy to be restored. This accounts for their joy when they saw Christ reinstating humanity in their midst and "human nature was reunited to the Principalities and the Powers and the Thrones and the Dominations in a great celebration given there for all." [9]

In the creation of the Church the angels behold the new universe in which the new man is created. "The foundation of the Church is the creation of a new universe. In her, according to Isaias, a new heaven and a new earth are created. In her is formed a different man, in the image of Him who created him. And just as he who looks upon the world of sense and grasps the wisdom which is manifest in the beauty of beings rises by means of visible things to the invisible, even so he who contemplates the new cosmos of the creation of the Church sees in it Him who is and will become all in all." [10]

The Book of Job shows the choirs of angels breaking forth in cries of great joy at the sight of God casting the foundations of the earth (38:4-7). With an even greater joy they greet the establishment of the Church, the new creation, and the formation of the new man who is created in her, the created reflection of uncreated beauty.

II. THE HEAVENLY FLOCK

The joy of the angelic creation in seeing Christ lead humanity back into heaven at the Ascension is expressed in the Fathers by other Biblical images. One of the most important

[8] *Hom. in Ps. 2.*
[9] *Serm. Nat.*, PG 44, 1049 C-1052 A.
[10] *Hom. in Cant.*, 13.

is that of the lost sheep. There is a whole tradition, with Irenaeus as its first witness, [11] but actually going back much further, which sees this sheep as human nature and the flock which the Good Shepherd leaves behind to set out in search for the sheep as the worlds of the angels. Origen sets it forth frequently. [12] Methodius of Philippi writes: "We must see in the ninety-nine sheep a representation of the Powers and the Principalities and the Dominations whom the Head and Shepherd has left behind to go down and seek out the one lost sheep." [13] And Cyril of Jerusalem says: "The angels are numerous. They are the ninety-nine sheep, whereas humanity is only one sheep." [14] Likewise Gregory of Nyssa: "We, mankind, are the lost sheep, we who by our sins have strayed from the hundred spiritual creatures." [15]

Christ, returning with the lost sheep on His shoulders, is the Word of God who has assumed human nature and leads it back into heaven at the Ascension. "He lifts the lamb entirely upon His shoulders. And the lamb borne upon the shoulders of the shepherd, that is, by the divinity of the Lord, becomes one with Him, being thus lifted up." [16] The parable tells us that there is "more joy in heaven over one sinner who repents than over ninety-nine just who have no need of penance" (Luke 15:7). This is the joy of the angels —that is, for the Fathers, of the ninety-nine sheep which the Shepherd left behind to set out in search of the stray sheep, and who now greet Him with joy as He returns with it. "When the sheep was found by the Good Shepherd all

[11] *Adv. haer.*, 3, 19, 3.
[12] *Comm. in Gen.*, PG 12, 102; *Hom. in Num.*, 19, 4: *Hom. in Gen.*, 13, 2.   [13] *Conv.*, 3, 6.   [14] *Cat.*, 15, 24.
[15] *Adv. Ap.*, 16. See also Hilary, *Comm. in Matt.*, 18, 6; Ambrose, *Exp. in Luc.*, 7, 210.
[16] *Ibid.*

the choirs of [heavenly] sheep broke forth with cries of gladness, according to the word of the Lord." [17]

Gregory of Nyssa has developed this theme at great length. "The full number of the angels adore Him who comes with the name of First-Born. They exult at the recalling of men by which, thanks to Him who has become the First-Born among us, we are called back to the original grace. For there is great joy among the angels over those who have been saved from sin." This joy of the angels at the return of the lost sheep is inaugurated at the Ascension, but will not reach its fulness until the Second Coming, "toward which they are constantly moving and ever waiting for us, until the lost sheep shall be rejoined to the full number of the sheep-fold. It is we who are the lost sheep, human nature, which the Good Shepherd has saved in becoming the First-Born among us. But now, above all else, in a heartfelt thanksgiving for us, the angels present their adoration to Him who, by His First-Born, has called us who have strayed far from the Father's hearth." [18]

This text is most rich in the allusions that have been woven into it. The basic theme is that of the heavenly Shepherd of the angels, who abandons the ninety-nine sheep, the worlds of the angels, to set out in search of the lost sheep, which is humanity. The Father's hearth alludes to the parable of the prodigal son. And the choirs who celebrate his return are those of the angels, [19] for whom something is lacking inasmuch as their unity is not yet restored.

Gregory Nazianzen develops the same theme. "In your mind has Christ belittled Himself because He has hum-

---

[17] *Hom. in Cant.*, 12. The word for herd is ἀγελῶν, a play with the word for angels, ἀγγέλων.

[18] *Contra Eun.*, 4. See also *ibid.*, 12; *Hom. in Eccl.*, 2.

[19] See Hilary, *Tract. Ps.* 149. Tertullian discusses this interpretation (*De pud.*, 7, 11), a fact which proves its antiquity.

bled Himself for you; because, as the Good Shepherd
who gives His life for His sheep, He has come for the lost
sheep, into the hills and mountains where you were sacri-
ficing, and found it straying there? Because He is the one
who, having found it, took it upon His shoulders, upon
which He also took the Cross and, having taken it up, led
it back to the life which is above, and, having made it rise
together with Him, has reunited it to the number of those
who were left behind? Because He has lighted His lamp
(that is, His flesh) and swept out His house (that is,
cleansed the world of sin) and once again found the
drachma (that is, the image of the divine) destroyed by evil
passions, and, having found it, has called together His
friends (that is, the angels) to make them partake of His
joy just as He made them the associates of His redemptive
plan?" [20]

Just as the image of the lost sheep mingles with that of
the prodigal son in Gregory of Nyssa, here it mingles with
that of the lost drachma. But then all three parables are
symbolical of the same mystery. It makes little difference
whether the angels are the friends of the woman who found
the drachma, the ninety-nine sheep who greet the return of
the Shepherd, or the choirs who celebrate the return of the
prodigal son. What matters is the Gospel idea that the
angels rejoice at the salvation of humanity. And Gregory
Nazianzen shows them associated with the lowliness of
the Nativity before being admitted to the joy of the Ascension. The two mysteries are always bound together.

III.   THE FRIENDS OF THE BRIDEGROOM

There are many other images which describe this same reality of the angels' joy. Thus, Gregory of Nyssa sees a figure

[20] *Or. Theoph.*, 14.

of it in the exultation of the daughters of Jerusalem welcoming young David in his victory. It is the figure of "the entire spiritual creation uniting itself, as in the harmony of one choir, with men who have conquered sin." [21] But one of these images is more important than the rest because it is connected with one of the most remarkable representations of the role of the angels, that of the friends of the Bridegroom in the Canticle of Canticles. This symbolism seems to go back to the Jewish tradition itself. In any case it appears before Origen in the works of Hippolytus. [22] Origen himself uses it several times.

The role of the friends of the Bridegroom is to conduct the Bridegroom to his Bride and to withdraw from them at once. Their joy is complete when their task is accomplished and the Bride is with the Bridegroom. That is the joy of John the Baptist: "He who has the bride is the bridegroom. But the friend of the bridegroom, who stands and hears him, rejoices exceedingly at the voice of the bridegroom. This my joy, therefore, is made full" (John 3:29). There is nothing left for the friend but to withdraw. "He must increase, but I must decrease" (John 3:30). This seems an allusion to the Canticle of Canticles. The friends of the Bridegroom are those who have prepared the ways of the Lord, who have led humanity to Him. Origen sees in them the prophets and the patriarchs of the Old Testament and John the Baptist, the last among them.[23]

But this is also true, and eminently so, of the angels. It is they, Origen writes, who are the friends of the Bridegroom, who have instructed his Bride—that is, the people of God— during the time of their engagement. We have seen that in respect to their role in the Old Testament. What, then, is

[21] *Hom. in Ps. 6.*
[22] *Comm. in Cant.,* 12.
[23] *Comm. in Jo.,* 6, 7.

their joy when they hear the voice of the Bridegroom—that
is, when they see the Word of God who has joined Himself
to humanity by the Incarnation, leading it into the house
of His Father at His Ascension, after having purified it in
the blood of the Cross. St. Paul was the first to apply this
symbolical wedding of Genesis and the Canticle to the
"mystery of Christ and the Church" (Eph. 5:32), describing the beauty of the Church, the new Bride, appearing now
before her groom "glorious, not having spot nor wrinkle"
(Eph. 5:27).

The angels, the friends of the Bridegroom, are united in
this nuptial mystery of the Ascension. Gregory of Nyssa,
connecting the parable of the servants who awaited the return of their master and the theme of the friends of the
Bridegroom, shows the angels waiting for the Lord to lead
the Church, His Bride, into the house of His Father. "It is
the angels to whom the Gospel precept compares us. Be like
unto men who await their master returning from the marriage feast. They awaited the return of the Lord from the
marriage feast, keeping close to the gates of heaven, constantly watching for Him so they would 'be ready to open
the gates for the Lord as He came from His wedding feast
to enter into supracosmic blessedness, 'like the bridegroom
who leaves his wedding chamber,' after having united Himself, in the regeneration of the sacraments, to the virgin
who had prostituted herself on idols—that is, with us, having restored our nature in all its virginal integrity. The
wedding feast is over, the Church is united to the Word
(for according to the word of St. John, 'he who has the
bride is the bridegroom') and has been admitted into the
wedding chamber of the sacraments; the angels await the return of the King, raising up the Church to share in His own
blessedness." [24]

[24] *Comm. in Cant.*, 11.

One can easily see how Gregory of Nyssa connects the theme of the king who has set out to celebrate his wedding, with that of the friends of the bridegroom. The marriage of Christ takes place upon the cross. That is where He is united to the Church. But after the wedding He returns to the house of His Father, leading the Church to which He is united. Here the role of the friends of the Bridegroom is no longer to prepare the wedding, but to accompany with their rejoicing His return into His Father's house. The preparation for the wedding was their role in the Old Testament; it was the role of John the Baptist. But their role in the Ascension is the return from the marriage; it is their exultation in seeing the salvation of humanity accomplished, the salvation they had been longing for during the long delays of the Old Testament and for which they had prepared the way. They cannot help greeting it with joy and thanksgiving. Moreover, this marriage of the Word and the Church is accomplished not only in the Passion and the Resurrection of the Word; it continues, throughout all the reign of the Church, in the wedding chamber of the sacraments, through Baptism and the Eucharist which are a participation in it. Hence we must now study the role of the angels in the sacramental life of the Church.

6 ෩

The Angels and the Sacraments

If the mystery of salvation is accomplished substantially at the Ascension, when the Word leads the humanity to which He has united Himself into the house of His Father in the midst of the praises of the angels, this mystery has to put forth its effects until the Second Coming, through the erection of the Church. The angels are associates in this plan. The earliest Christian traditions show us the Church entrusted to an angel, just as was the people of God in the Old Testament. The *Ascension of Isaias* speaks of the "angel of the Christian Church," [1] and Hermas designates Michael as "the one who has power over this people [the Church]

[1] *Asc. Is.*, 3, 15.

and governs them." [2] Whatever may be the truth as regards the angel of the Church, which seems more a heritage of Judaism and not in entire accord with the sole overlordship of Christ, this much is certain: in a more general fashion tradition pictures the angels as watching over and serving the Church. This is already contained in the Epistle to the Hebrews (1:14). Hippolytus, in an allegory in which he compares the Church to a boat, writes, "The Church also has its sailors, on port and on starboard—that is, the holy angels who help her; she is always watched over and defended by them." [3]

This role of the angels begins with baptism. Baptism is the continuation of the great works of God in both Testaments. It is a new creation. It is a resurrection. It is also the anticipation of the judgment at the end of the world. The same angels who assist the Trinity in the accomplishment of its admirable works are at hand here too as witnesses full of amazement and servants full of zeal. Thus the *Shepherd* of Hermas shows them working on the construction of the Tower that is built upon the water: that is, the Church, which is established upon baptism. "The tower that you see under construction is the Church . . . It is built upon water because your life has been saved by water . . . [These six young men who are building it] are the angels of God, the first to be set up, to whom the Lord has delivered all creatures, to organize, build, and govern them. It is by them that the construction of the Tower will be ac-

[2] *Sim.*, 8, 3, 3. See Apocalypse 12:7-9, where Michael appears as the defender of the Church. The expression "angel of the Church" is found again in Gregory of Elvira, *Tract.* 16.
[3] *De Antichr.*, 59. "The command to surround Sion is given, it seems to me, to the divine powers who watch over the Church of God and over the holy people in the Church" (Eusebius, *Comm. in Ps.* 47; 50).

complished." [4] How could the angels, who are the associates
of all the works of God, be anything less in this work of
works, which is the Church?

Just as they were at the same time the instruments for
what was prepared and the witnesses of what was accomplished in the mysteries of Christ, so they are in baptism.
They play an active role in the preparations for it. Just as
the Apostles were sent visibly to the pagan nations, the
angels are sent invisibly to draw them to the Church. "There
are other angels who gather the faithful from all nations.
Let us think for a moment whether this is not true: just as
in a certain city, for example, when as yet no Christians have
been born, if someone comes in and begins to teach and
work and instruct and lead to the Faith, he afterwards becomes the leader and the 'bishop' of those whom he has
taught; so also the holy angels will in the future become the
leaders of those whom they have drawn together from different nations and made to advance by the work of their ministry." [5] Here we find once again the angels of the nations
and their missionary role. [6] Now that Christ is here, they try
to lead to Him the souls entrusted to them. The angels of the
nations become the angels of the Church. [7]

In fact, there is a very early tradition which sees angels
placed at the head of Churches to establish and govern
them. The foundation for this is in the first chapters of
John's Apocalypse, where there is question of the angels of

[4] *Vis.*, 3, 3, 3-4. See also *Sim.*, 9, 12, 7-8.
[5] *Hom. in Num.*, 11, 4.
[6] Eusebius remarks that this mission is also a battle against idolatry, that is, against the demons who hold souls captive, and that
the angels take part in this struggle in an invisible manner
(*Comm. in Ps.* 17). This struggle of the angels against the demons of paganism is described in the Apocalypse of St. John.
See also Eusebius, *Comm. in Is.*, 42.
[7] *Hom. in Num.*, 11, 5.

the seven Churches of Asia Minor. Origen can write in his turn. "One might say, following Scripture, that there are two bishops in each Church, one visible, the other invisible, and that both are busied with the same task." [8] The Fathers of the fourth century continue this tradition. St. Basil speaks of the holy angels to whom the care of the Churches has been confided. [9] And St. Gregory Nazianzen shares his belief: "The care of this Church has been entrusted to an angel. And other angels are in charge of other Churches, as St. John teaches in his Apocalypse." [10] The farewell he addresses to the angels of Constantinople when he leaves his diocese is well known; he begs them to keep away "every obstacle which would obstruct the path of his people towards the heavenly Jerusalem." [11]

The role of the angels of the Churches has its remote beginning in their mission toward souls who are still pagan. More immediately this role derives all its meaning from the preparation for baptism, the catechumenate. Once again we discover the relation of the angels with preparations. St. Chrysostom teaches that "the deacon invited the catechumens to pray to the angel of peace." [12] The Sacramentary of Gelasius contains a prayer for the catechumens where they beg God "that He vouchsafe to send His holy angel to preserve His servants and to lead them to the grace of baptism." [13] Origen develops the theme with his usual lively

[8] *Hom. in Luc.*, 13.
[9] *Comm. in Is.*, 1, 46.   [10] *Or.*, 42.
[11] *Ibid.* See also Hilary: "There are spiritual powers, called angels, who are set over Churches" (*Tract. Ps.* 129); Eusebius: "There are angels to whom are entrusted the Churches which Christ has established everywhere in the world" (*Comm. in Ps.* 90), and more exactly: "One particular angel is set over each single Church as a guardian" (*Comm. in Ps.* 47).
[12] *Hom. in II Cor.*, 2, 8.
[13] Wilson, *Gelasian Sacramentary*, p. 48.

manner: "Come, angel, receive him who has been converted from his former error, from the doctrine of the demons . . . Receive him as a careful physician; warm and heal him . . . Receive him and give him the baptism of the second birth." [14]

Origen clearly associates the angel not only with the preparation for baptism but with baptism itself. This idea is developed by Tertullian, who attributes to the angel a role of the first importance in the sacrament: "Cleansed in the water by the action of the angel, we are prepared for the Holy Spirit . . . Thus the angel set in charge of baptism makes ready the way for the coming of the Holy Spirit by the washing away of sins." [15] It would seem, from a reading of this text, that the baptized person is first of all purified in the water by the angel, and then consecrated by the Holy Spirit. [16] This strange theory is interesting only for the allusion it contains to the angel of baptism. [17]

The teaching of the Fathers goes no farther than to show the angels assisting at baptism. Origen writes: "At the time that the Sacrament of the Faith was administered to you, there were present heavenly Powers, the ministrations of the angels, the Church of the first-born." [18] Gregory Nazianzen also thinks that "the angels give glory to the baptism because of its relation with their own sparkling purity." [19] And Didymus of Alexandria shows them assisting at the sacrament: "On the level of the visible, the baptismal pool gives birth to our visible body by the ministry of the priests;

[14] *Hom. in Ez.*, 1, 7.
[15] *De bapt.*, 6.
[16] See Amann, "L'ange de baptême chez Tertullien," *Rev. Sc. Rel.*, 1921, pp. 206 f.
[17] St. Thomas later proves that the angels cannot be ministers of the sacraments in the proper sense of the word (*ST*, 3, 64, 7).
[18] *Hom. in Jos.*, 9, 4.
[19] *Or.*, 40, 4.

on the level of the invisible it is the invisible Spirit of God
who plunges ($\beta\alpha\pi\tau\iota\zeta\epsilon\iota$) both our body and our soul into
Himself and regenerates us with the aid of the angels." [20]
Thus both the earthly Church of the priests and the
heavenly Church of the angels are ministers of the regeneration operated through the Holy Spirit.

In other texts the joy of the angels after baptism is more
profoundly developed. For instance, in the writings of Cyril
of Jerusalem. When describing to the catechumens the splen-
dors of the vigil of Easter on which they will be baptized, and
after having spoken of the glowing night and reopened Paradise, he writes: "Now lift up the eyes of your spirit and represent before yourself the angelic choirs, Almighty God upon
His throne, His only-begotten Son to His right, and the ever-
present Spirit at their side, the Thrones and the Dominions
all performing their ministry, and each one of you achieving
his salvation. Hear it already with your ears. Long for this
blessed word which the angels will speak at the moment
when, like the stars of the Church, you will enter, your
bodies splendid in their whiteness and your souls sparkling
with a blinding light." [21] It is a solemn moment of the Pas-
chal vigil which is described here, that in which the newly
baptized entered into the church in white robes to the chant-
ing of Psalms. [22]

Ambrose in his treatise *On the Sacraments* celebrates this
same solemn moment which follows baptism and constitutes
the entrance into the heavenly Jerusalem amid the myriads
of angels: "After baptism, you began to advance. The angels
watched, they saw you draw near, and they suddenly beheld

[20] *De Trin.*, 2. See also Optatus of Milevis, *Schism. Donat.*, 2,
10: "The profession of faith takes place in the presence of the
angels."
[21] *Procatech.*, 15. See also *Catech.*, 1, 1; 3, 3.
[22] Psalm 31 is still sung at this ceremony in the Eastern Church.

the splendor of your state, which had formerly been blemished by the ugly stain of sin. Thus they asked, 'Who is this coming up from the desert, shining white?' (Cant. 8:5). The angels are lost in admiration. Do you want to know how great their admiration is? Listen to the Apostle Peter as he tells us that we have been given what the angels desire to look upon." [23] Thus the radiance of the newly baptized awes the angels. And Ambrose compares their wonder with the wonder they felt at the Ascension of Christ, for baptism is a sharing in the exaltation of Christ above the world of the angels.

As the angels preside over baptism, so they are equally present at every Christian assembly. "On the question of the angels the following is a necessary conclusion: If *the angel of the Lord shall encamp round about them that fear Him, and shall deliver them*; and if what Jacob says is true not only in his own case but also in the case of all those who are dedicated to the omniscient God, when he speaks of *the angel that delivereth me from all evils*: then it is probable that, when many are assembled legitimately for the glory of Christ, *the angel* of each *encamps* round each of *them that fear* God, and that he stands at the side of the man whose protection and guidance has been entrusted to him. Thus, when the saints are assembled together, there is a twofold Church present, that of men and that of angels." [24]

The synaxis includes readings and a homily. The angels assist at the first half, drawn, Origen tells us, by the reading of the Scripture which they delight in hearing. [25] He who delivers the homily should not forget that they are listening and judging it. "I have no doubt that there are angels in the midst of our assembly too, not only the Church in gen-

[23] *De sacr.*, 4, 2, 5. See also *De myst.*, 35-36.
[24] Origen, *De or.*, 31, 5 (ACW 19).
[25] *Hom. in Jos.*, 20, 1.

eral, but each church individually—those of whom it is said that 'their angels always see the face of my Father who is in heaven.' Thus we have here a twofold Church, one of men, the other of angels. If what we say is in conformity with both reason and the meaning of Scripture, the angels rejoice and pray together with us. And since there are angels present in Church—that is, in the Church which deserves them, being of Christ—women when they pray are ordered to have a covering upon their heads because of those angels. They assist the saints and rejoice in the Church. We indeed do not see them because our eyes are grown dim with the stains of sin; but the Apostles see them, as they were promised: 'Amen, amen, I say to you, you shall see the heavens opened and the angels of God going up and coming down upon the Son of Man.' And if I had this grace which the Apostles had, I would see the multitude of angels that Eliseus saw, when Giezi, standing right beside him, saw nothing." [26]

But the angels are present especially at the Eucharistic sacrifice. The Mass is, actually, a sacramental participation in the liturgy of heaven, the cult officially rendered to the Trinity by the full host of the spiritual creation. The presence of the angels introduces the Eucharist into heaven itself. They help to surround it with a sacred mystery. "The angels surround the priest," writes St. John Chrysostom. "The whole sanctuary and the space before the altar is filled with the heavenly Powers come to honor Him who is present upon the altar." [27] And elsewhere: "Think now of what kind of choir you are going to enter. Although vested with a body, you have been judged worthy to join the Powers of heaven in singing the praises of Him who is Lord of all." [28] "Behold

[26] *Hom. in Luc.*, 23.
[27] *De sac.*, 6, 4.
[28] *Adv. Anom.*, 4.

the royal table. The angels serve at it. The Lord Himself is present." [29]

Erik Peterson, in *The Book of the Angels,* has shown that the participation of the angels in the Christian cult made clear its official character. There is only one priestly activity, and that is Jesus Christ's. By it the whole of creation glorifies the Trinity. This is this same activity that is offered by the angels in heaven and the saints on earth. This participation appears in the New Testament, where the liturgy of the Church is presented as a participation in that of the angels. Thus, in the Epistle to the Hebrews 12:22-24, we read: "But you have come to Mount Sion, and to the city of the living God, the heavenly Jerusalem, and to the company of many thousands of angels, and to the Church of the first-born who are enrolled in the heavens, and to God, the judge of all, and to the spirits of the just made perfect, and to Jesus, mediator of a new testament, and to a sprinkling of blood which speaks better than Abel." As for the Apocalypse, it is the vision of the Christian Sunday worship that the visionary sees as prolonged in the liturgy of heaven.

The angels are associated with the different parts of the sacrifice. [30] Theodore of Mopsuestia shows them symbolized by the ministers who arrange the offerings upon the altar: "By means of the deacons who minister in what is being accomplished we can see in spirit the invisible Powers ministering as they assist in this ineffable liturgy." [31] Further on he adds: "You must realize that there is an image of the invisible Powers in this service that the deacons are charged with now, as they bear the offering for the oblation . . .

---

[29] *Hom. in Eph.,* 1, 3.
[30] See Clement of Alexandria: "The angels of God serve the priests and deacons in the ministering of earthly affairs." (*Strom.,* 7, 1; *Hom in Lev.,* 9, 8.)
[31] *Hom. Cat.,* 15, 24.

And when they have brought it in, it is placed upon the holy altar by the angels for the perfect fulfillment of the Passion. The deacons who spread the cloths upon the altar recall the burial linens; and those who, once the sacred Body has been produced, stand on either side and fan the air around it, represent the angels who remained by Christ all the while He was dead, to honor Him, until they had seen His Resurrection." [32]

It is easy to see how the display of the liturgy of earth is a visible reflection, an efficacious symbol, of the heavenly liturgy of the angels. This unity of the two cults is expressed by the liturgy itself in the Preface, where it invites the community of the Church to unite with the Thrones and the Dominations, the Cherubim and the Seraphim, to sing the angelic hymn of praise, the Thrice-Holy: "Reflect upon whom it is that you are near and with whom you are about to invoke God—the Cherubim. Think of the choirs you are about to enter. Let no one have any thought of earth (*sursum corda*), but let him lose himself of every earthly thing and transport himself whole and entire into heaven. Let him abide there beside the very throne of glory, hovering with the Seraphim, and singing the most holy song of the God of glory and majesty." [33] Elsewhere Chrysostom remarks that the *Gloria in Excelsis* is the chant of the lower angels. Even the catechumens are permitted to join in it. But the *Sanctus* is the chant of the Seraphim; it leads into the very sanctuary of the Trinity, and thus "it is reserved for the initiated, the baptized." [34]

Theodore of Mopsuestia also stresses this participation in

[32] *Ibid.*, 25-27.

[33] Chrysostom, *Adv. Anom.*, 4.

[34] *Hom. in Col.*, 3. 8. On the Trisagion as the hymn of the angels in the liturgy of the Mass, see Chrysostom, *Adv. Anom.*, 1, 6; Cyril of Jerusalem, *Catech.*, 23, 6.

the angelic liturgy in the Trisagion. This point is especially dear to the tradition of Antioch. "The priest here mentions all the Seraphim who raise this song of praise toward God, the same song that blessed Isaias heard through a divine revelation and transmitted in Scripture. This is the praise which we all assemble together to sing at the top of our voices, so that we sing the same hymns as the invisible natures . . . By this means we show the greatness of the mercy He has bestowed freely upon us. A religous fear fills our conscience, either before or after we have cried out, 'Holy!' " [35] This chant of the Seraphim expresses holy fear. It describes the awe felt by even the highest creatures in the presence of the infinite divine excellence. And this enables us to understand better the holiness of the Eucharist which leads us, with the Seraphim, into the presence of the All-Holy God, hidden only by the fragile species of bread and wine.

Finally, the presence of the angels in the Eucharist appears in the very act of offering the sacrifice. The Roman liturgy itself witnesses to this when it asks of God that "the offerings be borne by the hands of Thy Holy Angel unto Thy high Altar." [36] The Apocalypse already shows the angels, in their heavenly liturgy, offering "the prayers of the saints" under the appearances of "cups of gold filled with perfume" (5:8). This intercessory role appears in the prayer of all prayers, the central act of worship, the priestly activity of Christ. Thus Chrysostom can write: "It is not only men who raise this cry filled with holy awe, but the angels prostrate themselves before the Lord, the archangels pray to Him. Just as men cut palm branches and wave them before their kings to move them to think of love and mercy, so at this moment the angels present the very Body of their Lord as

[35] *Hom. Cat.*, 16, 7-9.
[36] See B. Botte, "L'ange du sacrifice," *Rech. Théol. Anc. Méd.*, 1929, pp. 285-308.

if it were a palm branch and they pray to Him for all humanity." [37]

This participation of the angels extends to the whole liturgical life and especially to the celebration of the Christian feasts. The mysteries of Christ are celebrated by the heavenly powers at the same time as they are by the Church on earth. Thus Gregory Nazianzen writes, regarding the Feast of the Epiphany, "Together with the shepherds glorify God; sing His praises with the angels; join the choirs of the archangels. Let this festive occasion join the powers of those in heaven and those on earth. For I am certain that they are rejoicing today and celebrating this feast together with us, since they are friends of God and man just as those whom David shows us rising with Christ after the Passion, going on ahead of Him and vying with each other to lift up the gates." [38]

The last sentence is an allusion to Psalm 23, where tradition shows the Powers that ascend with Christ at His Ascension bidding the keepers of the gates of heaven lift their lintels to let the King of Glory enter. Just as they participated in His mysteries at the time of their historical accomplishment, the angels continue to be associated with their liturgical commemoration.

But it is Chrysostom who develops this idea to its greatest extent. He explains that, in order to lend greater splendor to the feast of the Ascension, he has invited the faithful to celebrate it in the *Martyrium* of Romanesia: "The angels are present here. The angels and the martyrs meet today. If you wish to see the angels and the martyrs, open the eyes of

[37] *Adv. Anom.*, 3. For Hilary the Eucharist is distributed to the faithful by the ministry of the angels: "This service is no doubt performed through the heavens, that is, by the angels" (*Tract. Ps.* 67). See J. Duhr, *Dict. Spirit.*, I, 591.
[38] *Or.*, 39, 17.

faith and look upon this sight. For if the very air is filled
with angels, how much more so the Church! And if the
Church is filled with angels, how much more is that true
today when their Lord has risen into heaven! The whole air
about us is filled with angels. Hear the Apostle teaching this,
when he bids the women to cover their heads with a veil because of the presence of the angels." [39]

And again, in regard to the Resurrection he writes: "It is
not only earth, but heaven as well which has part in today's
feast . . . The Angels exult, the Archangels rejoice, the
Cherubim and the Seraphim join us in the celebration of
today's feast . . . What room is there for sadness?" [40]

[39] *Serm. asc.*, 1
[40] *Serm. res.*, PG 50, 436.

7

The Guardian Angel

In the previous chapters we have considered the role of the angels in respect to the Christian community. But, in addition to this general role, they also have a mission toward each individual. Side by side with the angels of the Churches, there are angels of the faithful. It is on the guardian angels that tradition seems to be most constant and unyielding. "Among the angels," writes St. Basil, "some are set in charge of nations, others are companions of the faithful . . . It is the teaching of Moses that every believer has an angel to guide him as a teacher and a shepherd." [1] Basil bases his affirmation particularly on Genesis 48:16 and

[1] *Adv. Eun.*, 3, 1.

Matthew 18:10. Beyond a doubt, this is a doctrine which appears in Scripture. The most important texts are the Book
of Tobias, where the Archangel Raphael appears as the companion of the younger Tobias (Tobias 3:25), the text of
Matthew cited by St. Basil, where Christ says of the "little
ones" that their "angels in heaven always behold the face of
the Father" (18:10), [2] and finally the passage in the Acts
of the Apostles where there is mention of the angel of St.
Peter: "Then they said, 'It is his angel'" (12:15).

This doctrine appears in the earliest Christian texts. It is
found in Pseudo Barnabas, [3] in Hermas, [4] in Clement of
Alexandria, [5] who goes back himself to the *Apocalypse of St.
Peter*. Origen develops the doctrine to a great extent. "All of
the faithful in Christ, no matter how small, are helped by
an angel, and Christ says that these angels always see the
face of the Father who is in heaven." [6] Here Origen refers
to Matthew 18:10; elsewhere he refers to Acts 12:15. [7] He
also writes: "We must say that every human soul is under
the direction of an angel who is like a father." [8] The Fathers
of the fourth century profess the same doctrine. For St. Basil
"an angel is put in charge of every believer, provided we do
not drive him out by sin. He guards the soul like an army." [9]

[2] See J. Hering, "Un texte oublié, Matt. 18:10," *Mélanges
Goguel*, 1950, pp. 95 ff. On Judaism, see Philo, *De conf. ling.*,
27-28; *Life of Adam and Eve*, 33, 1.
[3] *Pseudo-Barn.*, 18, 1.   [4] *Vis.*, 5, 1-4.
[5] *Ecl.*, 41, 48.   [6] *De princ.*, 2, 10, 7.
[7] *Hom. in Num.*, 11, 4; see also 20, 3.
[8] *Comm. in Matt.*, 13, 5.
[9] *Hom. in Ps.* 33:6. See also Gregory of Nyssa, *Hom. Cant.*, 7;
Hilary, *Tract. Ps.* 124; *Tract. Ps.* 137: "All the faithful are aided
by the services of these divine ministers according to what has
been written: 'The angel of the Lord surrounds those who fear
Him' (Psalm 33:8)": Eusebius, *Praep. Ev.*, 13; Gregory the
Wonderworker, *Pan. Orig.*, PG 10, 1061 BC.

This whole tradition is echoed in the *Summa Theologica* of St. Thomas, where a lengthy article is devoted to establishing the existence and function of the guardian angel. [10]

It is interesting to take up one or the other of the expressions which designate the guardian angel and which make it easier to understand his role. He is called "guardian" (phylax) or "guard" (phrouros). [11] There are also the terms "protector" (prostates) and "superintendent" (epimeletes) [12] and "overseer" (ephoros). [13] Another name is "assistant" (boethos). [14] Particularly interesting is the name "shepherd" (poimen). His guardian angel appeared to Hermas in the form of a shepherd. [15] Basil calls his "herdsman" (nomeus). [16] Eusebius gathers the different names together and says: "Fearing lest sinful mankind should be without government and without guidance, like herds of cattle, God gave them protectors and superintendents, the holy angels, in the form of captains and shepherds. His First-Born Son is set above all of these." [17]

The activity of the angels accompanies the entire life of man. But the question arises whether all men or only Christians have guardian angels. In other words, is the guardian angel given at birth or only at baptism? Origen was familiar with both opinions and shows that each of them has Scriptural authority. [18] The matter still finds a place among the disputed questions of Stephen Gobar in the sixth century. St. Thomas devotes an article to it in the *Summa*, where he cites the passage of Origen. [19] The conclusion which St. Thomas reaches, moreover, is that toward which tradition

---

[10] *ST*, 1, 113.   [11] Eusebius, *Comm. in Ps.* 47.
[12] Eusebius, *Dem. Ev.*, 4, 6.
[13] Basil, *Ep.*, 2; Gregory Nazianzen, *Or.*, 13, 27.
[14] Basil, *Sp. Sanc.*, 13, 29.   [15] *Vis.*, 5, 4.
[16] *Adv. Eun.*, 3, 1.   [17] Eusebius, *Dem. Ev.*, 4, 6.
[18] *Comm. in Matt.*, 13, 27-28.   [19] *ST*, 1, 113, 5.

leaned: that man receives a guardian angel at birth, but that this angel plays an entirely new role after baptism. An analogy with the angels of the nations earlier made Origen tend toward this solution.

Actually, the role of the guardian angel before baptism is quite similar to the role fulfilled by the angels of the nations. It is true that an angel has been given to each man at birth. That is a doctrine of long standing. [20] But, on the other hand, from the first day of his life the little child becomes the prey of the devil, whether this be due to Satan's rights over the race of Adam or whether the child has been dedicated to him through idolatry. [21] As a result, the guardian angel is almost powerless over him, just as over the nations. [22] That is why the guardian angels were waiting for the help that would come to them from God. The coming of Christ reverses the situation. "You too were the lot of some prince. Then Jesus came and snatched you from the perverse power. Indeed, each of us has an adversary who seeks to draw us into the ranks of his own leader." [23] But now, thanks to Christ, the good angels are more powerful, able to defend the child who is, as it were, newly entrusted to them by Christ. [24]

As a matter of fact, Christ entrusts the newly baptized to their angels in a very special way. The role of guide, as we have seen, begins with the catechumenate and continues after baptism. Hermas insists on the role of the angel among

[20] Clement of Alexandria, Ecl., 50; Tertullian, *De an.*, 37, 1; Origen, *Comm. Jo.*, 13, 49; Methodius, *Conv.*, 2, 6.
[21] Tertullian, *De an.*, 39, 1.
[22] "If I belong to the Church, no matter how small I may be, my angel is free to look upon the Face of the Father. If I am outside the Church, he does not dare." (Origen, *Hom. in Luc.*, 35).   [23] *Ibid.*
[24] See Basil, *Comm. in Is.*, 8, 207; Origen, *Comm. in Matt.*, 13, 28; Severian of Gabala, *Hom. bapt.*, PG 13, 432 B.

THE ANGELS AND THEIR MISSION

the neophytes. He sees the many stones that are set into place in the building of the Church and explains: "Those that are put into their place in the construction of the Tower . . . are those who are new in the faith, but constant. They are formed by the angels in the doing of good, because no wickedness has been found in them." [25] Origen writes in turn: "When a man has received the Faith, Christ who has redeemed him by His blood from his evil masters entrusts him, since hereafter he is to believe in God, to a holy angel who, because of his great purity, always sees the face of the Father." [26]

Among the faithful those who have higher offices in the Church are the object of a very special protection. "If angels have been delegated by the God of the universe to those who have only their own personal lives to regulate and are to do nothing for the common good, how much more will they do for those men to whom the care of the whole earth has been entrusted! The Virtues of heaven are always with those who are charged with such offices." [27]

This doctrine, too, was first expressed by Origen. "The Apostles have the angels to assist them in the accomplishment of their ministry of preaching, in the completion of their Gospel work." [28] This does not refer only to the participation of the angels in the missionary work, but also to the guardian angels of the Apostles: "There is an angel of Peter just as there is an angel of Paul and of the other lesser ministers." [29]

Among the functions which the guardian angels exercise toward those entrusted to them there are some which have been already mentioned. Such is in particular the role of

---

[25] *Vis.*, 3, 5, 4.   [26] *Comm. in Matt.*, 13, 28.
[27] Chrysostom, *De laud. Paul.*, 7.   [28] *Hom. in Num.*, 11, 4.
[29] *Ibid.* See Eusebius, *Comm. in Ps.* 90; *Comm. in Ps.* 47 (which alludes to the angel of Peter, Acts 12:15).

"instructor," in virtue of which they are the messengers of inspiration to souls. They begin this mission among the pagans entrusted to them in order to lead them to the Faith; they continue it among the catechumens, then among the neophytes, and throughout the spiritual ascent up to the threshold of union with God. But there are many other functions attributed to them by the Fathers: they protect the soul against troubles from within and without; they reprimand and punish the soul that turns aside from the right way; they assist it at prayer and transmit its petitions to God. These three functions are designated by the Fathers under three titles given to the guardian angel. He is the angel of peace (Chrysostom), the angel of penitence (Hermas), and the angel of prayer (Tertullian).

Among these names for the guardian angel, that of "angel of peace" is especially venerable. [30] The expression appears in the Jewish apocalyptic literature, where the angel of peace is the one who accompanies Henoch and explains the meaning of his visions. [31] The expression had entered into the liturgy, as can be seen from a passage in St. John Chrysostom: "Learn now that there are angels of peace. Listen to the deacons, who frequently repeat in their prayers: 'Pray to the angel of peace.' " [32] As a matter of fact, it can be found in the *Apostolic Constitutions*, in the prayers which follow the dismissal of the catechumens: "Rising up, let us sing the mercies of the Lord. Let us pray to the angel in charge of peace." [33] The expression is found again in St. Basil, to

[30] The expression can be found in Isaias 33:7, in Jerome's translation.

[31] *Hen.*, 52 ,5; 53, 4; *Test. Aser.*, 6, 6; *Test. Dan.*, 6, 5.

[32] *Serm. asc.*, PG 50, 444 A.

[33] *Const. ap.*, 8, 3. See also *Hom. in Col.*, 1, 3: "We speak, invoking the angel of peace." Earlier there is a reference to the guardian angel.

designate the guardian angel who protects the voyager: "We pray to God who is well disposed toward men in order that He might give an angel of peace as a companion to protect us." [34]

In these passages the angel of peace is charged with the protection of the one entrusted to him. Since this protection may concern dangers from without, he is invoked by voyagers. Thus the Archangel Raphael was the traveling companion of Tobias. But it is especially a matter of protecting the soul against the devil. Accordingly, the angel of peace is especially invoked by the catechumens who are particularly exposed to the attacks of demons trying to hold them back. But these attacks beset even those who have been baptized, and the angel defends them too. Origen applies a verse from Psalm 90 to the Christians: "For he hath given his angels charge over thee; to keep thee in all thy ways." (Psalm 90:11). He comments: "For it is the just who need the aid of the angels of God, so as not to be overthrown by the devils, and so that their hearts will not be pierced by the arrow which flies in the darkness." [35]

This role of the angels was particularly stressed by St. Hilary. "In the warfare we carry on to remain strong against the evil powers," he says, "the angels are our helpers." [36] This assistance of the angels is bound up with man's weakness. "There are angels of little children who look upon the face of God every day. These spirits have been sent to aid the human race. For our weakness is such that, if the guardian angels had not been given to us, we could not resist the many and powerful attacks of the evil spirits. To this

[34] Ep., 1, 11. See also Comm. in Is., 13, 260: "Those who labor to attain salvation for us, neighbors and companions, are the angels of peace"; Gregory of Nyssa, Hom. Theod., PG 46, 745 C; Eusebius, Comm. in Is., 33.
[35] Hom. in Num., 5, 3.   [36] Tract. Ps. 65.

end we had need of a higher nature. We know that this
is so from the words with which the Lord strengthens Moses,
trembling in his fear, 'My angel will go before thee.' That is
why God has taken out these spirits from among his
treasures, and has given through them an aid to human weakness, so that this divine assistance might help us against the
powers of this world of darkness to attain the heritage of
salvation." [37]

Here Hilary merely takes up and comments on the text of
the Epistle to the Hebrews concerning the angels "sent for
service, for the sake of those who shall inherit salvation"
(1:14). And in interpreting the "winds" of Psalm 134 as
angels, he does nothing more than imitate what the Epistle
to the Hebrews had done for those of Psalm 104 (Hebrews
1:7). Gregory of Nyssa connects this doctrine to the vision
of Eliseus. [38] "Eliseus has taught us clearly that our human
weakness is protected by the assistance of angels and that
in all our perils, provided faith remain with us, we are defended by the aid of the spiritual Powers." [39]

But the assistance of the angel of peace is not only a protection against dangers. It is also a positive aid. Thus the
Gospel of Luke shows an angel comforting Christ in His
agony. The angels bring interior peace into the soul. Hermas,
accordingly, mentioned among the characteristics of the
good angel that he is "gentle and peaceful." Gregory of
Nyssa writes that "the Lord of the angels procures life and
peace through his angels for those who are worthy." [40] This
facet of the activity of the angels is cast in sharp relief by
St. Athanasius in the *Life of St. Antony,* in opposition to
the turmoil into which the demons throw the soul: "The
vision of the angels works softly and peaceably, awakening
joy and exultation." [41]

[37] *Tract. Ps.* 134.   [38] 4 Kings 4:15-17.   [39] *Tract. Ps.* 137.
[40] *Comm. in Cant.,* 14.   [41] *Vita Ant.,* 35.

This idea is found again throughout the spiritual tradition. St. Ignatius writes in the "Rules for the Discernment of Spirits": "It is characteristic of God and His angels that in their activity they give true joy and spiritual exultation, while removing the sadness and affliction that the enemy excites." [42]

Early tradition also shows that the angels are not unfamiliar with penitence. Penitence includes a vast reality of which the sacrament of penance represents only a small part. This was particularly true in primitive Christianity, which knew only public penance for grave sins. Here again the teaching of the Fathers continues that of Judaism, for in the Jewish apocalyptical literature there is an "angel of penance." In naming the four principal archangels, the Book of Henoch, after listing Michael, Raphael and Gabriel, mentions Phanuel, who is in charge of penance, for the hope of those who shall inherit life everlasting: "He puts the devils to flight and does not allow them to come into the presence of the Lord of the spirits, to accuse those who are on earth." [43]

Theirs, it will be noted, is a role both of conversion and of protection, both aspects of which will be found in later writers. So Clement of Alexandria speaks of the "angel of penance" in *Quis dives salvetur*. He shows the convert received by the angels and goes on to say: "He who has approached the angel of penance will have to repent no more when he leaves his body behind, nor blush when he sees the Lord coming with His armies." [44] But more important here is the *Shepherd of Hermas*. The entire book is an exhortation to penance, coming from the angel of penance, who is the Shepherd and who commands Hermas to hand on the message he is communicating to him. [45] The angel of

[42] *Exerc. spir.*, 329.   [43] *Hen.*, 40, 7-9.
[44] *Quis div.*, 42, 18.   [45] *Vis.*, 5, 7.

penance "holds the devil in his power," [46] just as he had
power over the devils in *Henoch*. Furthermore, he is the
messenger of hope for those who have been converted: "But
I entreat you, I the angel in charge of penance, to remain
firm in your proposal, whoever of you are such [simple and
innocent], so that your seed will not be rooted out forever.
For the Lord has put you to the test and entered your names
among ours." [47]

The role of the angel of penance becomes more precise
in Origen, where there is no longer question of a general
message, but of a real activity on the part of the angel in
the soul of the sinner to induce him to repent. Origen has
just spoken of the role of bishops and priests, "who instruct
the sinner, reproaching him and rebuking him with severe
words. It happens too that we are instructed by our guardians and our patrons, by which I mean the angels to whom
has been confided the task of directing and guiding our
souls, as is said of the angel of penance, who, according to
the *Shepherd*, cares for us in order to correct us. Moreover,
we are subject to various forms of remonstrance. We are not
at first chastised by the Father of the family Himself, but
by the angels whom He has sent as masters over us with the
office of chastising and correcting each one of us." [48]

But penance is not only chastisement; it also includes the
remission of sins and the restoration of the soul to health.
Origen attributes to the angels a role in this healing process.
Interpreting the parable of the Good Samaritan as pertaining to the conversion of the sinner, he writes: "When he
was about to leave in the morning, he took two pennies from
the money he had with him, from his silver, and gave them
to the innkeeper, certainly the angel of the Church, whom

[46] *Mand.*, 12, 4, 7.   [47] *Sim.*, 9, 24.
[48] *Sel. Ps.*, 37. See Rahner, "La pénitence chez Origène" *Rech.
Sc. Rel.*, 1950, pp. 81 and 88.

he commands to look after [the sick man] carefully, and nurse him back to health." [49] Elsewhere, comparing the resurrection of Lazarus to that of the sinner, Origen remarks that the body of Lazarus, after leaving the tomb, is still bound with bandages: "One might ask to whom Jesus said 'Loose him.' It is not recorded as being said to the disciples, nor to the crowd, nor to those who are with Mary. Because of the words, 'Angels drew near and ministered to Him,' and because of the symbolic character of the passage, one might suppose that it is other than these who are addressed here." [50] Here it is the completion of penance, the liberation of the soul from the bonds it has contracted with sin, which is reserved to the angels. [51]

Another name for the guardian angel is "angel of prayer." In the Apocalypse the angels present the prayers of the saints to God. This is true not only of liturgical prayer, but of private prayer as well. This doctrine is already found in the Old Testament, where the Archangel Raphael is one of the "seven holy angels who offer the prayers of the saints" (Tobias 12:15). [52] Clement of Alexandria speaks of "the angels who assist in the offering of prayers," [53] and he realizes that, even when man is praying alone, his prayer is joined to the choirs of angels. [54] Tertullian recommends that the Christians do not sit while praying, out of respect for "the angel of prayer who is at our side." [55]

Origen distinguishes the general presence of the angels

[49] *Hom. in Luc.*, 34.   [50] *Comm. in Jo.*, 28, 8.
[51] See Rahner, *loc. cit.*, p. 281.
[52] See Bietenhard, *op. cit.*, pp. 133-135. Philo of Alexandria does much to develop the teaching of the intercession of the angels, as messengers of God to man and man to God (*De gig.*, 3-7; *De somm.*, 1, 141-142).
[53] *Excerpt.*, 27.   [54] *Strom.*, 7, 12; see also 7, 2.
[55] *De or.*, 16; see Cyprian, *De or.*, 32-33; see also Luecken, *op. cit.*, pp. 67 and 93.

with regard to the one who is praying and the special presence of the guardian angel. "In the same way we must suppose that the angels who are the overseers and ministers of God are present to one who is praying in order to ask with him for what he petitions. The angel, indeed, of each one, even of the little ones in the Church, always seeing the face of the Father who is in heaven and beholding the divinity of our Creator, prays with us and cooperates with us, as far as is possible, in what we seek." [56] This participation of the guardian angel in prayer, his union with our supplication, comes up frequently in Origen. The Christian has nothing to fear from the devil, because "the Angel of the Lord shall encamp round about those that fear Him and he shall deliver them; and his angel, who constantly sees the face of the Father in heaven, always offers up his prayers through the one High-Priest to the God of all. In fact, he himself joins in the prayers of the one entrusted to his care." [57]

Thus the angel circulates between the soul and heaven. "We readily admit . . . that they rise upwards carrying the prayers of men . . . and come back down bringing to each one what he desires of the goods that God has appointed them to administer to the objects of their loving kindness." [58]

One outstanding point in the early tradition is the teaching that man has at the same time an angel and a demon within him, just as the nations have their angels and their devils. That was the teaching of Pseudo Barnabas, [59] who

[56] *De or.*, 11, 5 (ACW 19).
[57] *Contra Cels.*, 8, 36.
[58] *Ibid.*, 5, 4. See also *Hom. in Num.*, 11, 5; *Hom. in Lev.*, 9, 8. Hilary has this testimony to give: "There is positive grounds to the teaching (auctoritas absoluta) that the angels preside over the prayers of the faithful. They offer to God every day the prayers of those who have been saved" (*Comm. in Matt.*, 18, 5). See also *Tract. Ps. 129.*
[59] *Pseudo-Barn.*, 18, 1.

relates it to the doctrine of the two ways, that of good and that of evil. The angel draws the soul toward good, the devil toward evil. This is the doctrine of the discernment of spirits in root form. [60] Hermas insists even further on this point: "There are two angels for each man: one of justice and one of wickedness . . . The spirit of justice is mild and reserved and meek and peaceful. When he enters into your heart, he speaks at once with you of justice and modesty and temperance and kindness and pardon and charity and paternal love. As often as these thoughts arise in your heart, know that the spirit of justice is with you . . . Now learn the works of the spirit of wickedness too. First of all, he is irritable and bitter and rash, and his works are evil . . . When you recognize his works, depart from him." [61]

Origen inherits this doctrine from Hermas, as he himself says explicitly. Through him it passes on to Athanasius and then to a whole spiritual tradition. "The *Shepherd* [of Hermas]," he writes, "makes the same statement, saying that two angels accompany every single man; and whenever good thoughts come into our mind, it says they are put there by the good angel; but if they are otherwise, it says that that is the impulse of the evil angel. Barnabas also makes the same statement, in his *Letter*." [62] Here Origen is only the representative of an older tradition, but he makes this tradition an essential part of his spiritual teaching. "All men are moved by two angels, an evil one who inclines them to evil and a good one who inclines them to good." [63] And again: "What I say of every single province I think ought to be believed as well of every single man. For everyone is influenced by two angels, one of justice and the other of

[60] See *Manual of Discipline* (Qumran), 4, 2-14.
[61] *Mand.*, 6, 2, 2-5.
[62] *De prin.*, 3, 2, 4.
[63] *Hom. in Luc.*, 35.

iniquity. If there are good thoughts in our heart, there is no doubt that the angel of the Lord is speaking to us. But if evil things come into our heart, the angel of the evil one is speaking to us." [64]

Thus man finds himself in the middle of a spiritual combat between the powers of light and the powers of darkness. This great theme, which St. Ignatius is to develop in the contemplation of the two standards, is already in Origen. [65] St. Athanasius devotes a considerable part of the *Life of St. Antony* to it. [66] Gregory of Nyssa expounds it clearly, connecting it with the idea of the guardian angel. "After our nature had fallen in sin, we were not abandoned in our fall by God, but an angel, one of the beings who have an incorporeal nature, was set up to aid the life of each of us. The destroyer of our nature, in his turn, did just the same by sending us an evil, pernicious angel to the detriment of human nature. It now depends upon man, who finds himself between two angels, each one seeking to lead him in a different way, to make the one triumph over the other. The good angel presents his spirit with the fruits of virtue, everything that those who do good see in hope. The other angel holds up before him the pleasures of earth, pleasures which hold no hope for the future, but pleasures which can captivate the minds of the foolish when they are seen and enjoyed in the present." [67]

Man lives, therefore, in the middle of a supernatural world, a spectacle, as St. Paul says, to both men and angels. That is what makes St. Hilary say: "Everything which seems empty is filled with the angels of God and there is no place that is not inhabited by them as they go about their minis-

[64] *Ibid.*, 12.
[65] *Hom. in Num.*, 20, 3.
[66] *Vita Ant.*, 29-43.
[67] *Life of Moses*, PG 44, 337 D-340 A.

try . . . If the fear that someone might come upon him un-
expectedly often holds a person back from the commission
of some sin he has been planning, how should the Christian
act, and not merely act but even think and desire, when he
realizes that every part of him is the dwelling place of such
a number of spiritual powers? When we are overcome by
some evil will, should we not tremble before the presence
of the choirs of angels that surround us? If, in fact, the angels of the little children see the face of the Father every
day, we must certainly fear their testimony, knowing that
they are at the same time near to us and present before God.
And we must just as certainly fear the devil and all his witnesses who make themselves present in an instant from one
end of the earth to the other." [68]

But this presence of the angels not only keeps man back
from committing sin; it makes him tend toward good as well.
"The prophet hastens to accomplish the action which the
spiritual natures contemplate spiritually. He knows that his
entire life is enacted in full view of the angels and he wants
to please the spiritual beings by contemplating spiritual
realities." [69]

[68] *Tract. Ps.* 118.
[69] *Tract. Ps.* 137.

8

The Angels and the Spiritual Life

The assistance of the angels which is given to the soul at
baptism is to continue throughout the whole course of its
life. Not even sins can suppress it. They can only sadden the
angel of the soul. [1] But angels do not merely protect the soul
against the attacks of the devil; they also try to make it
progress in the spiritual life. This is the first aspect under
which the spiritual life appears in relation with the angels.
On the other hand, following a teaching which has its source
in the Gospel itself, the spiritual life appears as an imitation
of the life of the angels and a participation in their life. It
reintroduces the soul into the angelic creation. But the fact

[1] Origen, *Hom. in Luc.*, 35.

remains that the ascension of the soul leads it even higher than the angels. The Christian mystery is the exaltation of humanity above the sphere of the angels. This mystery, which is true first of all of Christ Himself, is true of the whole of human nature which He leads along with Him as a retinue.

The angels, then, appear first of all as aiding the soul in its spiritual ascension. [2] Certainly it is from God that all the spiritual gifts come, but He communicates them through the intermediary of the angels. Clement of Alexandria shows spiritual goods being transmitted from their source in God down to man through the hierarchies of the angels: "It is from one principle from on high working in accord with the will [of the Father] that the first order of things are dependent, and then the second and the third. Then, at the other end of creation there are the blessed orders of angels. And thus going from one to the other, but always springing from the One and by the power of the One, the hierarchy comes down even to us." [3] This hierarchical conception is taken up and systematized by Pseudo-Dionysius: "The higher order, closer by its very dignity to the secret sanctuary, mysteriously initiates the second order. This in turn, composed of the Dominations, the Virtues, and the Powers, reveals the mysteries in a less secret way than the first hierarchy, but less openly than the third. Thus it is the order of Principalities, Archangels, and Angels to whom the office of revealer belongs. It is this order which, through all the

---

[2] "It is through the ministry of the angels that we have received the opportunity to ascend to the things on high" (Hilary, *Tract. Ps.* 120); "They are lever-bars, sent for the service of those who are to receive the heritage of salvation, to raise them to the heights of virtue" (Gregory of Nyssa, *Life of Moses*, PG 44, 384 B).

[3] Clement of Alexandria, *Strom.*, 7, 2.

degrees of its own internal constitution, presides over the
hierarchies of men, in order that their spiritual elevation
toward God will be effected in a harmonious fashion." [4]

Pseudo-Dionysius, continuing the earlier tradition, divides
this activity of the angels into three functions: purification,
illumination, and unification. [5] The purifications administered by the angels are those in the depths of the soul con-
suming the blindness of the flesh that prevents the soul from
becoming united to God. Thus Scripture shows the Seraphim purifying the lips of the prophet Isaias (Is. 6:7).

Gregory of Nyssa applies a verse of the Canticle of Canticles to this activity of the angels, "The guards who go about
the city struck me" (5:7). These guards, he says, are the
ministers of the one who watches over Israel. [6] The blows
they strike the soul and the veil they lift from it are a figure
of the purifying operations they accomplish in it. Gregory
compares the verse of the Canticle to the passage in Isaias:
"Just as here the bride says that she is struck and wounded
by the guards and robbed of her veil as well, there, in the
same manner, in place of the veil, it is the heavenly lintel
which is drawn up so that the realities in the sanctuary can
be contemplated without obstruction. In place of the guardians, there is mention of the Seraphim. Instead of a rod,
there are burning coals; instead of blows, a bright fire." [7]

Pseudo-Dionysius likewise describes this purifying activity,
connecting it with the Seraphim; but, in conformity with
his hierarchical view, he explains that it is through the intermediary of lower hierarchies that the Seraphim perform this
activity. "The Theologian learned that purification and all
the functions of the Divine Lordship, reflected through the
degrees of higher essences, are shared by all the other essences in proportion to the part each of them plays in the

[4] *Hier. coel.*, 9, 2.   [5] *Ibid.*, 10, 1.
[6] *Hom. in Cant.*, 13.   [7] *Ibid.*

divine work . . . That is why he attributes the property of purifying by means of fire first of all after God Himself to the Seraphim." [8] The purifying operations come from God as their one source; but the principal ministers are the Seraphim, who perform the purifications through the lower angels.

United to the function of purification is that of illumination. This role of the angels is particularly dear to St. Thomas of Aquinas, who studies the modalities in it. Before him Gregory Nazianzen had described it. [9] It is in his writings that the role of light receives a position of importance: "God is the supreme light, inaccessible and ineffable, incomprehensible to the mind, unspeakable by any word, illuminating all of the spiritual creation. He is in the world of intelligibles what the sun is in the visible world. The more we purify ourselves, the more we know Him; and the more we know Him, the more we love Him . . . The second in the order of light is the angel, an emanation or participation of the first light, illuminated by turning toward it and following it. It shares in this illumination, according to the degree of its nature, unless perhaps the degree of its nature is determined by its illumination." [10] The last sentence marks his hesitation between Origen's conception of hierarchy according to grace and the conception which will prevail in Pseudo-Dionysius of a hierarchy of natures.

Now, illuminated by God, after having turned toward Him, the angelic powers illuminate in their turn those who are lower than they. If someone were to say something in

[8] *Hier. coel.*, 13, 4.
[9] Origen had already written: "There had to be angels who are in charge of holy works, who teach the understanding of the eternal light, the knowledge of the secrets of God and the science of the divine" (*Hom. in Num.*, 14, 2).
[10] *Or.*, 40, 5.

praise of the angels, he might say that they are illuminated from on high by a most powerful illumination, each in his own manner, in accord with his nature and rank. They are so informed and imprinted by the source of all beauty that they themselves become lights and thus illuminate others with the light which is derived and communicated to them from the first light; for they are servants of the divine will and penetrate forcefully everywhere both by nature and by grace, leading all to unity under the sole command of the Creator of all." [11] In these texts a descending hierarchical order can be observed, in accordance with which the light of the Trinity is communicated through the various angels to man. That is the doctrine which Pseudo-Dionysius develops at length.

What he really does is systematize this concept more vigorously and in particular set it in relation with the doctrine of the nine choirs of angels. Here the whole *Celestial Hierarchy* could well be quoted, but there is one passage which sums up its teaching: "The oldest rank among the intelligent beings who surround God, initiated into the mysteries by means of illuminations which have come to them from the Source and Principle of all illumination and toward whom they rise without the office of any intermediary, receive the office of purifying, illuminating, and finishing. After them, in proportion to the nature of each, the second order, and after the second the third, and after the third the hierarchy of men, in accord with a divine system of proportions, each rises hierarchically toward the Source and Goal of all harmony. These orders are each to serve as revealers and messengers for the orders which precede them." [12]

Through these purifications and illuminations the angels lead the soul to the peaks of the spiritual life. In revealing

[11] *Ibid.*, 28, 31.   [12] *Hier. coel.*, 10, 1-2.

the beauty of God, they awaken in the soul a more burning thirst for union with Him. Thus they are the friends of the Bridegroom in a new sense, leading the soul to the wedding chamber where it will celebrate its mystical marriage with the Word. It is these angels that Gregory of Nyssa sees in the Canticle of Canticles: "After having testified to the beauty of the soul, the friends of the Bridegroom who make ready His spotless wedding chamber and form the escort of the pure Bride, show her the beauty of the royal couch to stir up in her an even greater desire for a divine life and a holy union with Him." [13] Thus, the activity of the angels accompanies the soul all during its ascent. "The souls make their way toward the Almighty in happiness and joy, protected and escorted by the angels." [14]

But the soul is associated with the angels in its progress toward God not only in being assisted by them but also in that the spiritual life assimilates it to the life of the angels. This theme can be found already in the Gospel, where it is said that the "elect will be like the angels of God in heaven" (Matt. 22:30). The perfect life is an anticipation of this final eschatological transformation. [15] The spiritual life reintroduces the soul into heavenly familiarity with the angels. Thus Origen writes: "But set forth, nor be afraid of the desert solitude. Soon even the angels will come to join you." [16] This theme is developed by Methodius of Olympia in the *Banquet of the Twelve Virgins* and is taken up again by Gregory of Nyssa. For him, the spiritual life makes the

[13] *Hom. in Cant.*, 6.
[14] Methodius, *Conv.*, 7, 9.
[15] On the spiritual life, and the monastic life in particular, as an angelic life, see A. Stolz, *Théologie de la mystique*, pp. 110 ff.; L. Bouyer, *Le sens de la vie monastique*, 43-68; Agnes Lamy, "Bios angelikos," *Dieu vivant*, VII, 59 ff.
[16] *Hom. in Num.*, 17, 4; E. Bettencourt, *Doctrina ascetica Origenis*, pp. 30 f.

soul enter into the world of the angels. Thus he writes of his sister Macrina: "Living in the flesh, she was not held down by the weight of the body, but her life was light and ethereal and she walked upon the heights with the Powers of heaven." [17] And likewise of his brother Basil: "Having risen above the zone of this sensible universe, he would abide in the world of intelligibles and converse with the Powers of heaven, without any carnal weight to impede the progress of his spirit." [18]

But this return to a place among the heavenly Powers signifies a participation in their being. The soul that rises toward God is declared to be like to the angels. "The beauty of the soul is likened to the cavalry which defeats the Egyptians, that is, the army of the angels [Cant. 1:8]." [19] And elsewhere, commenting on the comparison between the Bride and an army drawn up in battle array, he writes: "These armies in battle array are those where the Powers are in perpetual sway, where the Dominations rule forever, where the Thrones are established never to be changed, where the Principalities abide independent. Since these powers have been ordained by God and since the order of the powers above this world always remains without confusion, with no evil ever attacking their good order, the soul, in their image, does everything with moderation and thus provokes as much admiration for her as the orderly battle array." [20]

What allies the soul to the angels is its detachment from the life of sense. "Scripture admonishes our souls to contemplate the stable nature of the angels, so that our stability in virtue will be fortified by their example. For since it has been promised us that the life after the resurrection will re-

[17] PG 46, 972 A.
[18] *Ibid.*, 813 D. See J. Danielou, *Doctrine spirituelle de Grégoire de Nysse*, pp. 101 ff.   [19] *Hom. in Cant.*, 3.   [20] *Ibid.*, 15.

semble the condition of the angels—and He who made that promise does not lie—it follows that already our life in this world should be in conformity with that which will follow, so that living in the flesh and finding ourselves upon the battlefield of this world, we ought not to live according to the flesh and join forces with this world, but we should already begin to conform with the life we hope for after that of this world. That is why the Bride exhorts the souls to turn toward the powers of heaven, in imitation of their detachment, to attain to the purity of the angels." [21]

This is the whole of the doctrine. Men are destined to participate after death in the life of the angels; the spiritual life makes them anticipate this condition; finally it is the *apatheia* (impassibility) which constitutes the imitation of the angelic purity. This occurs again and again in Gregory. One more image expresses this return to the angelic nature, that of the night-watch, which makes man like those angels whom Scripture calls Night-Watchmen. "The soul illuminated by the Word becomes a stranger to the slumber of illusion. It is a type of angelic life to which He thus introduces us." [22] More particularly, virginity is an anticipation of the life of the angels. The idea is developed by Methodius of Philippi: "The wings of virginity lead to the borders of angelic life." [23] Gregory of Nyssa repeats it: "Since the Lord has told us that life after the resurrection is like that of the angels and since a characteristic of angelic life is that it knows nothing of marriage, those who practice virginity are already imitating the incorporeal beings." [24]

[21] *Ibid.*, 4. See also Theodoret, *Graec. affect. cur.*, 3.
[22] *Ibid.*, 11.   [23] *Conv.*, 8, 2.
[24] PG 46, 381 A. Introduced into the life of the angels by asceticism, the soul can then take part in the liturgy of the angels (Eusebius, *Comm. in Ps.* 102). See E. Peterson, *Theologische Traktate*, p. 257.

In those authors in whom the theme of an angelic hierarchy appears, this idea of an assimilation to the life of the
angels takes on the form of a successive assimilation to the
different orders of the angels. The soul takes on the form of
each of them in the measure that it rises in the hierarchy.
This doctrine appears in Clement of Alexandria; according to
his curious conception of things, the soul is instructed first
of all by the angel who is immediately above it, then it takes
on the nature of that angel and is instructed by the next angel of a higher rank. [25] Under this form the doctrine cannot
be held, since it supposes that natures are not fixed. St.
Thomas, however, keeps the idea of an "assumption" of the
soul into the various angelic orders, on the plane of grace.
Actually, according to his doctrine, the grace of the angels is
proportionate to their nature, whereas that of men is not. [26]
The grace of any man, therefore, can lead him first to the
degree of grace of one angelic order and then to that of a
higher order.

Thus the angels accompany the soul throughout the
length of its spiritual life. Still, this should not obscure one
final point; namely, that their role remains above all one of
preparation. They lead the soul toward Christ, but leave it
there alone with Him. They are the friends of the Bridegroom who withdraw when the Bridegroom is there. Origen
was the first really to emphasize this characteristic of the
action of the angels, the fact that it is concerned with the
beginnings of the spiritual life: "Look and see if it is not
above all the children, led by fear, who have angels; and if
in the case of the more advanced it is not the Lord of the
angels who says to each of them: 'I am with you in tribulation.' To the extent that we are imperfect, we have need of
an angel to free us from evils. But when we are mature and

[25] *Eclog.*, 57.
[26] *ST*, 1, 108, 1.

when we have passed the time for being under teachers and masters, we can be led by Christ Himself." [27]

Here Origen stresses a general aspect of the doctrine of the angels, their relation with beginnings and preparations. It is they who prepared the path of Christ in the Old Testament; they are the friends of the Bridegroom whose joy is perfect when they hear the voice of the Bridegroom and who leave the Bride alone with Him; it is they who, as the Gospel teaches, have a particular relationship with children. So their role remains connected with the beginnings of the spiritual life. They draw the soul to good by noble inspirations and they give it a horror of sin. Thus they dispose it to receive the visitation of the Word. But they withdraw before Him. In the course of its spiritual ascent, the soul passes first of all through the angelic spheres, but it goes beyond in order to arrive at the realm of God. The whole mission of the angels is to lead souls to the King of the angels and then to disappear before Him.

This idea that the soul, after having entered into the sphere of the angels, goes through it and passes beyond it, appears in a beautiful extract from Clement of Alexandria, who recalls the role of the angels as friends of the Bridegroom whose only duty is to lead the soul to the threshold of the wedding chamber: "The priest, upon entering within the second veil, would take off his mitre beside the altar of incense. He himself would enter further in silence, with the Name engraved upon his heart. Thus he showed that the setting aside of the golden mitre which had become purified and light by the cleansing, as it were, of the body, was really a setting aside of the heaviness of the soul . . . He puts aside this light mitre when he has come with it inside the second veil in the world of the intelligible, that is, the

[27] *Comm. in Matt.,* 12, 26. See also *Comm. in Jo.,* 1, 25; *Hom. in Num.,* 11, 3; 14, 3. See E. Bettencourt, *op. cit.,* pp. 24-28.

second veil, alongside the altar of incense, beside the ministers of the prayers that are being offered, the angels. Then
the naked soul, having become in reality a highpriest, is
thereafter moved directly by the Word . . . Passing beyond
the teaching of the angels, she goes on to the knowledge and
understanding of things, no longer merely betrothed but
dwelling with the Bridegroom." [28]

This beautiful text is a fine résumé of the doctrine: the
soul, having entered into the angelic world through the il-
luminative life, then passes through it and enters into the
unitive life, which is that of the Bride, and there it is moved
directly by the Word. Gregory of Nyssa develops the same
theme, but in relation to a different image, that of the
Bride in the Canticle who begs each of the guards of the
city, the angels, for her Bridegroom: "In spirit she runs
through the intelligible world of the Principalities, the
Powers and the Thrones to see if her Beloved is among
them. But they keep silent. Then, leaving all that she has
found, she recognizes Him whom she is seeking." [29] It is
after having left the angels behind that the soul takes hold
of God. Beyond the images that they leave upon her she
reaches Him as He really is, in the darkness of faith, through
the grasp of love.

That is how the angels assist in the ascent of the soul.
They see it leaving behind the darkness of sin, rising up to
them by the life of grace, ascending even beyond them in
the glory that the Word of God conferred on humanity
when He united Himself to it. Gregory of Nyssa, commenting on this verse of the Canticle, describes their admiration:
"Could it be that we too shall rise with the perfect dove
who goes up toward the heights and that we too shall hear
the voice of the friends of the Bridegroom admiring the

[28] *Excerpt.*, 27; see also *Strom*, 7, 3.
[29] *Hom. in Cant.*, 6.

beauty of her who comes up from the desert? What seems to me to cause the astonishment of the friends of the Bridegroom is that first of all they had seen this beautiful soul, but beautiful insofar as it was among women, and that, after having thus compared her beauty to gold set with silver stipples, now they admire her as a column of incense smoke rising from the desert. The very fact that they inquire among themselves about her always appearing under a different form from the one she formerly had is the greatest praise for the soul which progresses in holiness." [30]

So the soul rises, from transformation to transformation, up to union with God, amid the worlds of angels who cry out in their amazement. "*Quae est ista?* Who is this soul?" Christ rose toward His Father in the same way, amid the choirs of angels, who said one to another in admiration and amazement, "*Quis est iste?* Who is this man?" In reality it is the selfsame mystery. The ascension of the soul is a form of the ascension of Christ. St. Ambrose, we recall, pictures the angels wondering at the ascent of the newly baptized from the baptismal pool and crying out, "*Quae est ista?*" [31] Similarly, the angels who assist at the ascension of a martyr cry out, "*Quis est iste?*" [32] Throughout all the planes of the Christian mystery, therefore, there is one same ascension through the midst of all the choirs of the angels.

[30] *Ibid.*
[31] *De sacr.*, 4, 5.
[32] Origen, *Hom. in Judic.*, 7, 2.

9

The Angels and Death

After having assisted men throughout the course of their earthly life, the angels play an outstanding role at the moment of death. Biblical tradition and Greek tradition join in this teaching. The New Testament shows Lazarus "carried by the angels to the bosom of Abraham" (Luke 16:22). The Greeks were familiar with *psychopompoi*, or soul-escorting angels, who accompany the soul, after its death, toward its heavenly abode.[1] The Christian liturgy retains this reference to the angels in the Mass for the Dead, the Offertory of the Roman Mass imploring that "Michael, the standard-bearer, may lead us forward into the holy light, promised of

[1] Cumont, *Les vents et les anges psychopompes, Pisciculi,* p. 70.

old to Abraham and to his seed." This is an echo of the Jewish traditions on the role of Michael as the guide of the dead. Another echo of them is the Epistle of Jude, which shows Michael struggling with the devil over the body of Moses (1:9).[2] Still another text in the liturgy for the dead petitions that "the angels lead thee into Paradise."

It is hardly astonishing, then, that the Fathers of the Church picture the angels assisting the soul at the moment of death and leading it to Paradise. Tertullian writes in *De Anima:* "When, by the force of death, it [the soul] is snatched from the weight of the flesh that closed it in, it trembles with excitement to see the face of the angel, the summoner of souls, realizing that its eternal abode has been prepared."[3] The same doctrine often appears in Origen.[4] Pseudo-Justin writes: "Immediately after the soul leaves the body, there follows a separation of the just from the sinners. Then they are led by the angels to the places they are deserving of."[5] Gregory of Nyssa sees in the young David, who was welcomed after his victory by the daughters of Jerusalem, a figure of the soul being received by the angels after having triumphed over the adversary by death; and he relates the episode to that of Lazarus: "The choir of the daughters of Jerusalem is the journey made with the angels."[6] Chrysostom says: "If we need a guide in passing from one city to another, how much more will the soul need someone to point out the way when she breaks the bonds of flesh and passes on to the future life."[7]

That is why the prayers for the dead invoke the assistance

[2] See *Test. Aser,* 6, 4-7; *Life of Adam and Eve,* 40-43.
[3] *De an.,* 53.
[4] *Hom. in Num.,* 5, 3; *Comm. in Jo.,* 19, 15.
[5] *Quaest. orth.,* 75.
[6] *Hom. in Ps. 6.*
[7] *Hom. in Laz.,* 2, 2.

of the angels. These prayers present a twofold aspect. On the one hand, the guardian angel of the soul is asked to accompany it during its voyage to heaven. In the *Life of Macrina* Gregory of Nyssa puts on the lips of his dying sister a prayer which is filled with Biblical and liturgical reminiscences. In it is found this passage: "Send to my side the angel of light to guide me to the place of rest, where the water of repose is found in the bosom of the Patriarchs."[8] The connection with the bosom of the Patriarchs recalls the story of Lazarus.

St. Ephrem sees the angels "taking up the soul (after it has left the body) and carrying it through the upper air."[9] This belief is responsible for the numerous representations of angels on funeral monuments. These continue up to the Middle Ages. The front gate of Saint-Trophime at Arles pictures a soul being carried by an angel into the bosom of Abraham.[10] In the Dialogues of St. Gregory the Great, so filled with allusions to the invisible world, the angels often come to serve the saints at the hour of their death. The witnesses who were assisting at the death of the pious Stephen saw the angels "without being able to express what they had seen because they were so struck with fear."[11] The death of the saints appears as a mystery full of sacred terror. The hymns of the angels fill the soul with so divine a joy that it does not notice the sufferings of death.[12] And during its voyage toward heaven, the angels scatter the demons who try to bar the soul's advance.[13]

Secondly, the angels of heaven, the guardians of Paradise,

[8] PG 46, 984 D.
[9] *De sec. adv.*
[10] Leclerq, *Anges*, DACL, I, 2127.
[11] *Dial.*, 4, 19.
[12] *Ibid.*, 14.
[13] Ephrem, *Sec. adv.*

are asked to permit the soul to enter there. Here once again we find that there are two groups, the angels of earth and the angels of heaven. Just as the liturgy invokes the angels who lead the soul into Paradise, it also contains allusions to those who welcome the soul there. The *Apostolic Constitutions* contain a prayer for the dead which is drawn up in this manner: "Cast thine eyes upon thy servant. Forgive him if he has sinned and make the angels well-disposed toward him." [14] St. Ephrem pictures the confusion of a man confronted by the heavenly powers, "when the armies of the Lord show themselves and when the divine commanders bid him leave the body behind. He shakes, he trembles at the unaccustomed sight of these figures, these choirs which he has never seen before. All of us, trembling, say to each other: 'Pray that your soul leave your body in peace. Pray that it find the angels well-disposed.' " [15] This is an echo of the liturgical prayer of the *Constitutions*. Gregory of Nyssa insists on this point to demonstrate the necessity of Baptism: "I do not know whether, once it has left the body, the angels will receive the soul which has not been illuminated and adorned with the grace of regeneration. For how could they, if it does not bear the seal and has no sign of its quality? Probably it is borne upon the air, wandering and vagabond." [16]

This twofold aspect of the relation between death and the angels is expressed in the prayer which an early apocryphal writer puts into the mouth of St. Joseph at his death: "But now, O my Lord, let your holy angel keep close to my soul and my body until they separate from each other without pain. Do not permit that the angel who was attached to me since the day you formed me up to now should turn

[14] *Const. ap.*, 8, 41.
[15] *Ibid.*, 275.
[16] *Serm. bapt.*, PG 46, 424 B.

toward me, his countenance smouldering with anger, when we are on our way along the road that leads to you. Do not allow my soul to be stopped by the keepers of the gate and do not put me to shame before your fearful tribunal. Do not loose against me the floods of the river of fire in which all souls are purified before they see the glory of your divinity, O God, You who judge each one in truth and justice." [17]

All the aspects of the angelology of death are gathered together here: the angels help the soul escape the sufferings of death; the guardian angel accompanies it and assures it a peaceful journey; he defends it against the demons who want to stop it; the angels set in charge of the gate of heaven welcome it. One final point will be noted, the river of fire. That is the Christian doctrine of purgatory, and it is shown in relation to angelology. If the soul which the angel is leading is not entirely pure, it has to be purified before appearing before the face of the all-holy God. It has to receive a baptism of fire, which complements the effects of the baptism of water. But this baptism is given by the angels, according to the ancient traditions which pass down the doctrine of purgatory. Thus the *Apocalypse of Paul* speaks of a man lifted up in a vision into the heavenly abodes: "Behold! A river with its waters. I say to the angel, 'What is it?' He answers, 'If anyone is impure or unholy, but repentant, once he has left his body behind, he is led forward first to adore God, and then by the command of the Lord he is handed over to the Angel Michael, who baptizes him in the river and then leads him to the city of God.'" [18] The guardian angels of the heavenly Paradise retain the soul until it has been purified of its sins in the river of fire.[19]

[17] *Hist. Jos.*, 13.   [18] *Apoc. Paul*, 22.
[19] See C. M. Edsman, *La baptême de feu*, pp. 64 ff.

This doctrine is often presented under a different form. The angels are shown examining the merits and demerits of the souls who present themselves before the gates of heaven. They are somewhat like customs officials at the gates of cities.[20] This concept, which has its origins in paganism,[21] persists in the Oriental Church. From this same source comes the idea of the weighing of souls by the angels, a representation so frequent in medieval architecture. This examination of souls is often attributed to evil angels: it is they who accuse the soul and prevent its entry into heaven.[22] That was the figure of Satan in the Book of Job. But this role is also ascribed to good angels. "The choir of angels is our witness, the Powers of heaven are waiting for us lovingly, to see when and in what manner we return from this battle, how many spoils we have carried off. They watch with attention, they make a most thorough search to see which of us are carrying the greatest quantity of gold or silver or precious stones . . . There will be a thorough search when we have arrived there, to discover what each of us is bringing; and according to the measure of what each one has brought . . . will be determined the dwelling that he deserves." [23]

Actually, both the bad angels and the good angels have their parts to play. The first group keep count of the demerits and hold the soul back until it has been acquitted of them. The second group count the merits and determine a fitting place for the soul. This furnishes the grounds for the debate between Michael and Satan over the lot of the soul, an idea which was popular in the Middle Ages.

The second part of the angels' role is to lead the holy

[20] Origen, Hom. in Luc., 23.
[21] Cumont, Etude sur le symbolisme funéraire, pp. 76 ff.
[22] Origen, Comm. in Rom., 7, 12.
[23] Hom. in Num., 25, 5.

souls into heaven once their justification is accomplished.[24] They flock eagerly to the men who are already perfect, especially to virgins who already lived, in spirit, the life of an angel. "It is contrary to the nature of the wings of virginity," writes Methodius, "to hang heavily downward toward earth. Rather, they should bear one up to the heights in the pure ether and into a life near that of the angels. That is why after the signal has been given from on high for the departure from this earth, those souls who have made a sincere and faithful consecration of their virginity to God are the first to receive the reward of their combat, being crowned with the flowers of incorruptibility. For it has been said that as soon as the souls have left the world, the angels come to meet the virgins and address a great many words of welcome to them, and then accompany them into the heavenly fields where they have long desired to enter even though they have but imagined them, and from a distance, while they were living in their bodies." [25] This is found again in Eusebius: "The virgins will not walk toward the King; they will be carried. For others will be leading them—the angels of God, who will carry these noble souls up to make their journey easier." [26]

But it is the martyrs, bathed in their own blood and not in need of purgatory, for whom the angels reserve their most splendid welcome. Origen insists especially on this point in his *Exhortation to Martyrdom*. First of all, in relation to I Corinthians 4:9, he shows the angels assisting with open admiration at the struggles of the martyrs. "A great multitude is assembled to watch you when you combat and are called to matryrdom. It is as if we said that

[24] Hilary, *Tract. Ps.* 58.
[25] *Conv.*, 8, 2.
[26] *Comm. in Ps.* 44. See also Ephrem, *Hymn. Parad.*, 6, 24; Beck, *op. cit.*, pp. 60 f.

thousands gather to watch a contest in which contestants of outstanding reputation are engaged. When you are engaged in the conflict you can say with St. Paul: 'We are made a spectacle to the world and to angels and to men.' The whole world, therefore, all the angels on the right and on the left, all men, both those on the side of God and the others —all will hear us fighting the fight for Christianity. The angels in heaven will rejoice with us." [27]

Here Origen does nothing more than develop a point from the New Testament. It is St. Paul who first saw the martyr as a wondrous spectacle to amaze the powers of heaven.

If the angels of heaven assist with admiration at the struggles of the martyr, how much more joyfully will they welcome him when he arrives as conqueror at the threshold of Paradise. "If these two [the Cherubim and the flaming sword] guard the way to the tree of life, they do so in order that no one unworthy may pass by it and come to the tree of life. The flaming sword will keep back them that, on the one foundation which has been laid, Christ Jesus, have built with wood or hay or stubble, and that wood which is most flammable and burns most fiercely, apostasy. The Cherubim will receive them that could not be overcome by the sword of fire, because they have built nothing which it could touch, and will bring them to the tree of life and to all which God has planted . . ." [28]

This is a theme of frequent occurrence in the acts of the martyrs. An angel of heaven comes to seek them and lead them to paradise. It can be found already in the *Acts of Perpetua and Felicity*, in the vision of Saturnus: "We had undergone martyrdom and had left the flesh behind. Four

[27] *Exhort.*, 18 (ACW 19).
[28] *Ibid.*, 36 (ACW 19). Likewise Hilary, referring to the first martyr, Stephen (*Tract. Ps. 58*).

angels began to carry us toward the East. Their hands did
not even touch our bodies. Then we arrived at a vast place
which looked like an orchard with rose bushes and all kinds
of flowers. Here there were four other angels more brilliant
than the first. As soon as they saw us, they greeted us and
said to the other angels with great admiration, 'Behold
them! Behold them!' " [29]

More particularly, Origen shows the angels looking with
wonder at the ascension of a martyr, just as they did at that
of Christ: "Who could follow the soul of a martyr as it
passes beyond all the powers of the air [the demons] and
makes its way towards the altar of heaven? Blessed is that
soul which, by the crimson of its blood poured out in
martyrdom, puts to rout the ranks of the demons of the air
advancing toward it. Blessed is he of whom the angels shall
sing the prophetic words as he enters into heaven, 'Who is
this that comes up from Bosra?' " [30] All of tradition puts this
verse of Isaias into the mouths of the angels greeting Christ
as He rises to His Ascension, "His vestments dyed" with the
blood of His Passion.

Attention should be recalled to the passage of St. Ambrose
where he depicts the angels looking with wonder upon the
newly baptized rising from the baptismal pool, quoting the
verses of Psalm 23. The Ascension of Christ, baptism, and
martyrdom are three manifestations of one single mystery,
that of the introduction of humanity, bathed in its own
blood, into the House of the Father, amid the wonder of
the worlds of the angels.

This admiration has found in St. John Chrysostom a poet
who devotes a passage of great beauty to it: "Think then

[29] *Act. Perp.*, 11.
[30] *Hom. in Judic.*, 7, 2. Gregory of Nyssa presents "the angels
waiting on the death of martyrs in order to lead their souls
into their abodes" (*Serm. 40 Mart.*).

of that spiritual ladder which the Patriarch Jacob saw
stretching from earth to heaven. The angels were coming
down along it and the martyrs were going up . . . You have
often seen the sun rise in the morning, darting out purple-
tinted rays in every direction. Such were the bodies of the
martyrs: the crimson tide of their blood had flooded every
part of them as with rays of purple and illuminated their
bodies more than the sun lights up the heavens. The angels
gazed upon this blood with delight. The demons were
struck with fear, and the devil himself was trembling . . .
The martyrs go up to heaven, preceded by the angels and
surrounded by the archangels as by an escort . . . When
they have arrived in heaven, all the holy powers from on
high run forward and stand before them, trying to see their
wounds. They receive them with joy and embrace them.
Then they form an immense procession to lead them to the
King of Heaven, who is sitting upon a throne filled with
glory in the midst of the Seraphim and the Cherubim . . .
There they join the choirs and take part in the mystical
songs. If, still in their bodily nature, they were admitted into
the choir during the participation in the holy mysteries, to
sing the Trisagion with the Cherubim and the Seraphim—
and you who are initiated know that this is so—then how
much more fully will they participate hereafter in this
liturgy together with their heavenly companions!" [31]

This beautiful text gathers together the whole liturgy
which the angels perform for the martyrs in their ascension.
The angels of earth accompany them in their ascent and
form their escort. The angels of heaven come out before
them to welcome them. They lead them into the Holy of
Holies where the Trinity dwells in the midst of the Cheru-

[31] *Ibid.*; see also *Serm. Jul.*, 3. See Gregory of Nyssa, *Serm.
Theod.*: the martyr becomes a part of the choirs of the angels
and participates in their heavenly liturgy.

bim and the Seraphim. They have a share in their liturgy, even inside the sanctuary, and pass through all the spheres of angelic spirits, Angels of earth, Archangels, Seraphim, Cherubim. The ascension of the martyr realizes everything which the ascension of the mystic realizes spiritually, according to the teaching of Clement and Gregory of Nyssa. And it is easy to see that the Trisagion in the sacrifice of the Eucharist is a sacramental participation in the heavenly liturgy of the Cherubim and Seraphim. It is a liturgy into which the martyrs are introduced beyond the veils of the liturgy of earth.

10

The Angels and the Second Coming

But the ministry of the angels toward the men entrusted to them is not yet finished. If their souls are in heaven, their bodies are still awaiting the resurrection. During this time the angels keep watch over the tombs of the saints, preventing their profanation. Their role is, after all, to protect whatever is consecrated to God. This is shown by a number of Christian inscriptions on monuments: "Here rest Asclepias, Elpisias, and another Asclepias. I pray you in the name of the angel who tarries here that no one make bold to place another body with theirs." [1] This protection exercised by the angels over the bodies of the saints is an old belief

[1] See Leclerq, *op. cit.*, I, 2141-2144.

which dates back to Judaism and which has found its way into the New Testament. If the *Assumption of Moses* tells us that at the moment of Moses' death, "Josue saw his soul rising to heaven amid angels," [2] the Epistle of Jude shows "the Archangel Michael fiercely disputing with the devil about the body of Moses" (Jude 1:9).[3]

At the end of time, it is the angels who will be the ministers of the Lord at the resurrection of the dead. This activity of the angels at the Second Coming is one of the aspects of angelology which are most strongly attested by the New Testament itself. In the Gospel of Matthew Christ is announced as "sending forth his angels with a trumpet and a great sound, and they will gather his elect from the four winds, from end to end of the heavens" (Matt. 24:31). The First Epistle to the Thessalonians says that "the Lord himself with cry of command, with voice of archangel, and with trumpet of God will descend from heaven; and the dead in Christ will rise up first" (Thess. 4:16). The reapers who separate the good grain from the cockle "are the angels," sent by the Son of Man "at the end of the world, and they will gather out of his kingdom all scandals and those who work iniquity" (Matt. 13:40-41). The angels will assist at the last judgment: "But when the Son of Man shall come in his majesty, and all the angels with him, then he will sit upon the throne of his glory; and before him will be gathered all the nations, and he will separate them one from another" (Matt. 25:31-32). The angels thus appear associated with various moments of the eschatological drama; they are the ministers of the resurrection of the dead, the gathering together of the elect, and the separation of the just from the wicked.

[2] *Assumption of Moses*, 23.
[3] In the *Apocalypse of Moses* (40, 1-7) the angels care for the body of Adam after his death.

These various aspects are taken up and developed by tradition. Thus the *Second Sibylline Book*, which is Christian, shows the archangels shattering the gates of death, raising up the bodies, even those who have been drowned in the sea or those whom savage beasts have devoured.[4] A homily wrongly attributed to St. John Chrysostom shows the Archangel Michael "sounding his trumpet in the presence of Christ and waking those who have died from Adam to the end of time." [5] This same resurrection to the sound of angel trumpets is described by St. Ephrem, the great bard of the Second Coming: "Then the Lord will appear in the heavens like lightning with an unspeakable glory. The Angels and the Archangels will go on before His glory like flames of fire, like a mighty torrent. The Cherubim will turn their faces and the Seraphim will fly ahead crying out in fear: 'Arise, you who sleep. Behold the Bridegroom is coming.' Then the tombs will be opened and in the flash of an eye all the peoples will rise and behold the holy beauty of the Bridegroom." [6] Cyril of Jerusalem writes: "The Archangel will make a proclamation, saying to all men, 'Arise to meet your Lord, for the coming of the Lord is awe-inspiring.' " [7]

Side by side with the resurrection, the gathering of the nations is attributed to the angels, in accord with the treatise on eschatology. The *Second Sibylline Book* describes them gathering men in order to lead them before the throne of God.[8] Cyril of Jerusalem shows the angels leading the sinners: in the full sight of the armies of heaven, they will be unable to escape.[9] But they are also uniting the just: "The King of Glory will overlook none of His servants when He comes escorted by the angels to share the throne of His Father. Lest His elect be confused with His enemies, He

[4] *Second Sibylline Book*, 2, 214-235.   [5] PG 61, 775.
[6] *Sec. adv.*, 7, 11.   [7] *Cat.*, 15, 21.
[8] *Second Sibylline Book*, 2, 235.   [9] *Cat.*, 15, 22.

will send His angels with the sound of a trumpet to gather
the elect from the four directions. 'Come, blessed of My
Father,' He will say to those who will be carried upon the
clouds as upon carriages, gathered together by the angels." [10]
The same idea appears in Ephrem: "Then the angels will be
sent out in every direction, to gather together the elect
from the four winds, according to the word of the Lord." [11]
Here once again the outstanding characteristic of the missions of the angels is verified: just as they prepared the
hidden coming of the Lord, so they are the precursors of
His glorious Second Coming. "The angels go before Him
and the choir of the archangels forms His escort." [12]

As ministers of the preparation for judgment, the angels
are also witnesses to it.[13] Cyril of Jerusalem describes the
extraordinary magnificence which the presence of the immense multitude of angels lends the final judgment. The great
depths of the spiritual world, invisible up to now, except
to the eyes of faith, are suddenly made manifest: "Thus you
see, O Mortal, before what a multitude of witnesses you shall
enter into judgment. The whole human race will be present
there. Try to imagine all those who have existed since the
time of Adam to the present day. That is a great crowd,
but still it is little. The angels are more numerous. They
are the ninety-nine sheep, whereas humanity is the one sheep.

[10] *Ibid.*
[11] *Sec. Adv.*, 2, 3. See also Hilary, *Comm. in Matt.*, 26, 1: *Tract.
Ps. 146*; Eusebius, *Comm. in Ps. 49*: "God wants the saints to
be gathered together first."
[12] *Ibid.*
[13] According to Origen, these are in particular those angels who
have had the responsibility of human souls: "Every angel, at
the end of the world, will present himself for judgment, leading
with him those whom he guided, helped, and taught" (*Hom.
in Num.*, 11, 4). But this, in his mind, does not prevent the
angels from being judged as well.

After all, it is written that His ministers are a thousand times a thousand, not that this figure sets a limit to their multitude, but rather because the prophet could not express a larger number." [14]

The same presentation can be found in Ephrem. After depicting the angels and the archangels in their roles preceding the Second Coming, he describes them assisting at the judgment itself: "Then we shall see the innumerable armies of the angels take their place about their God. Then the works of each one shall be proclaimed and revealed before angels and men. Then the prophecy of Daniel will be fulfilled: 'I beheld till thrones were placed and the Ancient of days sat: his garment was white as snow, and the hair of his head like clean wool: his throne like flames of fire: the wheels of it like a burning fire. A swift stream of fire issued forth from before him: thousands of thousands ministered to him, and ten thousand times a hundred thousand stood before him' (Dan. 7:9-10)." [15] The text of Daniel is the common source of both Cyril and Ephrem. It shows the judgment as accomplished in the presence of an immense multitude of angels. The allusion to the river of fire is also noteworthy in that it is an important Scriptural source for the angelology of the Second Coming.

Finally, the angels are the executors of the sentence. The Gospel of St. Matthew already shows them as such, "gathering out of his kingdom all scandals and those who work iniquity, and casting them into the furnace of fire" (Matt. 13:42). The Apocalypse of Peter presents a detailed picture of this scene, frequently copied by others. The Sibylline Books describe this ministry of chastisement, but they also show the angels leading the elect into paradise after their resurrection: "All the others, all those who have looked for

[14] Cat., 15, 24.
[15] Sec. adv., 2, 3-4.

justice and acted according to what was right will be taken by the angels and led to a life of blessedness." [16] These eschatological views are frequently found in the older Christian popular literature, especially the apocrypha,[17] but they are also found among the Fathers. The description of punishment is met with,[18] but more frequently that of glorification. Here once again it is Ephrem who appears as the great visionary of the Second Coming: "Then the angels will come together from all sides and take up the holy and faithful people into the glory of the clouds above to their meeting-place with Christ." [19] Before him Origen depicted the angels escorting the risen souls into paradise: "When this tabernacle has been dissolved, and we have begun to enter into the Holies and pass on to the promised land, those who are really holy and whose place is in the Holy of Holies will make their way supported by the angels, and until the tabernacle of God comes to a halt, they will be carried on their shoulders and raised up by their hands. This the Prophet foresaw in spirit, when he said: 'For he hath given his angels charge over thee; to keep thee in all thy ways' (Psalm 90:11). But everything that is written in this Psalm applies to the just rather than to the Lord . . . Paul, treating of the same mystery, strengthens the belief that some will be borne upon the clouds by the angels when he says, 'Then we who live, who survive, shall be caught up together with them in the clouds to meet the Lord in the air' (1 Thess. 4:17)." [20]

[16] *Second Sibylline Book*, 2, 313-317.

[17] See Luecken, *op. cit.*, pp. 126-128.

[18] Eusebius, *Comm. in Is.*, 13; 21; 30.

[19] *Sec. adv.*

[20] *Hom. in Num.*, 5, 3. See also Eusebius, *Comm. in Is.*, 66: "The angels will lead the elect to their blessed end, when they will be lifted up, carried as was Elias on an angelic chariot, amid the rays of heavenly light."

Then for the last time, when the last enemy, death, has been overcome, and the Son is about to return all things to His Father, the angels who accompany Him now in the fulness of His supreme Ascension will make the heavens echo with their cry: "Rise up, everlasting gates, and the King of Glory will enter." "When the Son of God comes in glory and power and when He annihilates the wicked and conceited tyranny of the son of perdition by making known His presence and by the breath of His mouth, and when the spirits of heaven and the angelic servants of God accompany the Son of God and appear together with Him, then the powers of the heavens will be shaken, and these words will be accomplished: 'Rise up, gates of eternity, and the King of Glory will enter.' Where will He enter if not into the new world, the new universe? Even the invisible and incorporeal powers through whom the heavens are administered will be shaken from their permanent station. Heaven itself, the sun, the moon, and the stars will pass away; the heavens will open; the gates closed since the beginning of time will fold back and open to view the realities above the heavens." [21]

If the angels welcome the final establishment of the Church in the heavenly city with such great joy, it is first of all because of the disinterested love they bear for it, but also because of the advantages it will produce for them. In the first place, they will be freed from their service in a world that is not lasting. This is explained by St. Hilary when he applies to the angels the verse of the Epistle to the Romans on the *expectatio creaturae* (8:19): "Once they are all established in the blessed peace of eternity, the choir of the Virtues and the Powers of heaven will gather together to sing the praises of God. The vanity of this world has disappeared. The entire creation of

[21] Eusebius, *Comm. in Luc.* See also *Comm. in Is.*, 13.

the angels is freed from the great burdens of its ministry. Resting peacefully now in the blessed kingdom of eternity, they glorify their God in joy and peace, according to the words of the Apostle: 'For the eager longing of creation awaits the revelation of the sons of God. For creation was made subject to vanity' (Rom. 8:19-20). That is why creation sings a hymn for the liberation which has been promised." [22]

It is in this same eschatological sense that Hilary interprets the realities "into which the angels desire to look" (I Peter 1:12). "Freed from the obligations of their service, since they were before subject to the needs of service among men, the elements of creation enter into their rest. This desire for happiness long haunted them, according to the Apostle Peter, who says, 'The things which have been announced to you, and into which the angels desire to look.' The object of the angels' waiting and desire is the happiness of men. The elements of the divine creations are waiting for the state of our corruption to be changed; they desire to see accomplished what the Gospel promises. And once this promise is fully worked out, they will be called to give glory together with us for the gift of eternal happiness." [23]

St. Gregory of Nyssa insists upon a different aspect, the joy of the angels in seeing the unity of the spiritual creation restored: "Up until now creation groans and travails in pain, subject because of us to vanity, seeing in our fall a loss to itself, until the revelation of the sons of God, for which the angels never cease to wait in eager expectation for us— until the sheep which has been saved is reunited to the holy hundred fold. For we are the sheep, we whom the Good Shepherd, in becoming man, has saved. But then in a heart-

[22] *Tract, Ps. 148*, PL 9, 879 C. See Origen, *Comm. in Rom.*, 7, 4; Eusebius, *Comm. in Luc.*, PG 24, 597.
[23] *Ibid.*

felt sentiment of gratitude they will present their thanksgiving to Him who by His First-Born has called back the
straying sheep to the Father's hearth." [24] Then the perfect
liturgy will be established which will glorify the Trinity for
eternity. "When grace has reunited men and angels, they
will break forth into a great hymn of praise." [25]

On that day the joy of the friends of the Bridegroom will
be complete. They have sighed for His coming during the
long preparations of the covenants with Noe and Abraham.
They have greeted His appearance with a great joy and
exalted His glorious Ascension. They have put themselves
at the service of His redemptive work throughout the time
of the Church, to convert, illuminate, and unite mankind
to God. They have led to paradise the souls of the just
who were entrusted to them. They have kept watch over
their mortal remains. But they still await the day on which
the Bridegroom will come to look for His Bride, when her
beauty is finally perfect, in order to lead her into the House
of His Father for the eternal wedding feast.

"O dearly beloved, they burn to see the day of your
marriage—all the angels you have called from heaven, O
King. They will come, O Word, and they will carry with
them mighty gifts, in their spotless robes." [26]

[24] *Contra Eun.*, 4.
[25] *Hom. in Ps. 9.*
[26] Methodius, *Conv.*, p. 11.

Index of Citations